PRACTICALLY PAGAN

An Alternative
Guide to Gardening

PRACTICALLY PAGAN

An Alternative Guide to Gardening

Elen Sentier

MOON
BOOKS

Winchester, UK
Washington, USA

JOHN HUNT PUBLISHING

First published by Moon Books, 2021
Moon Books is an imprint of John Hunt Publishing Ltd., No. 3 East Street, Alresford
Hampshire SO24 9EE, UK
office@jhpbooks.net
www.johnhuntpublishing.com
www.moon-books.net

For distributor details and how to order please visit the 'Ordering' section on our website.

Text copyright: Elen Sentier 2020

ISBN: 978 1 78904 373 0
978 1 78904 374 7 (ebook)
Library of Congress Control Number: 2020947606

A CIP catalogue record for this book is available from the British Library.

Design: Matthew Greenfield

UK: Printed and bound by CPI Group (UK) Ltd, Croydon, CR0 4YY
Printed in North America by CPI GPS partners

We operate a distinctive and ethical publishing philosophy in
all areas of our business, from our global network of authors to
production and worldwide distribution.

Contents

About Me ...

This book is not just another version of organic and environmentally friendly gardening, it's about reconnecting with Nature. It leads you through the eight seasons of the Celtic pagan year, and gives you guidance on how to work with each season.

I'm a passionate gardener and have been gardening all my life. My dad was a gardener as well as an enginèer and in his spare time he grew our vegetables, fruit and flowers, and gave me my love of roses. Uncle Perce was the sort of gardener who won prizes at all the local shows and kept bees too, was a bee-listener, and showed me how to do that as well. Uncle Jack was a forester and woodsman who cared for the trees and forests where we lived, managed the woods and copses and large acreages of forest too for the local farmers and landowners. He knew intimately how plants work together, and how they work with the animals, insects and birds, indeed how the whole ecosystem works homogenously of itself. Much of what he taught me is nowadays the subjects of university degrees, as environmental science, but Uncle Jack knew from it his apprenticeship with his father, and grandfather before him. He passed it on to me.

Both my parents and most of our relations were followers of the Old Ways of Britain, Cunning Folk and Wise Women as we say in Britain, so I was brought up in all that, it was normal and just what one did. The old ways of our country are deeply entwined with love of, and care for, the land and all that lives and grows there. And there's no real feelings of ownership or separation. We know we don't own things but are guardian to them for a while.

The old ways are organic and magical, and really valuable to us today as we learn how to live with climate change. Gardening can show us how to reconnect with Nature.

My Pagan Perspective

This book gives you my own pagan perspective. As we say of ourselves, to get a roomful of pagans to agree on something is worse than herding kittens! We're all individual, have our own viewpoints, but one thing we agree on is the love of Mother Earth, of Nature, and the love of all the non-human beings with whom we share our lovely planet. This book comes from there. So, to garden as a pagan means learning to look at gardens – and indeed the whole natural world – with different eyes... eyes that see whole, that don't see us humans as separate from the natural world but as an integral part of it.

So, what comes into your mind when you hear the word *Pagan*? Maybe it's bloodthirsty Vikings setting Christian churches on fire; or perhaps heavy metal guitarists wearing silver pentacle necklaces; or it might be dark robed, bearded weirdos slaying goats in forests; or just something bizarre that likely involves worshipping the devil? Actually, there's only one word in that whole long sentence that relates to being Pagan ... and it's *forest*, not pentacle!

We're people of the land – that's what the word *pagan* means, it come from the Latin word *paganus* and that literally means *of the land*; so, we're people of the forest and hilltop, the valley and the rushing stream, the wild mountain and the wide moorland, the rivers, the seashore and the cliffs. We're people who love and work with Mother Earth.

We're a complete hotchpotch of peoples, there are pagans all over the world, in all different races and cultures and lifestyles. We have no one standard way of being, or set of rules, we all do it in our own way, and that too is all part of being *of the land*. The land here where I live is different to the land where you live, it needs different things, it's good at growing different plants, its water tastes different to yours, its weather and geology are different to yours. We hear lots about biodiversity nowadays – and I'm all for it. And diversity is vital for peoples and how they see the universe too.

We pagans have always been many different peoples, not all tramping along in step, or thinking in the same box, and we still are. Our ways are all about where we live, about the spirit of place of the land where we live, and spirit of the district, and of our own little plot that we're guardian to at the moment, as well.

Like people say nowadays about their relationship ... it's complicated! And so is living with the Earth, but my goodness it's fun. We're not alone, we have all of the natural world as our friends if we're willing to connect and communicate with them. Even if we're the only human person living in that house, we know we can – if we wish – be in contact with, and chatting with, all the spirits who live there along with us, and the local wildlife too. We know they will help us and so all we have to do is learn to ask, learn how to open up a conversation with them. Being pagan is all about that, all about connecting and conversing with the spirit world, and with all the natural world too. We often begin that by talking with our plants in the garden.

I live in the Welsh Marches, the borders between Wales and England, and hereabouts we call ourselves *wledig*. It's an old Welsh (Brythonic) word that also means *of the land*, just as the word pagan does. In the old stories you'll see it used as a title for our leaders, priests and kings, like the hero-king Macsen Wledig from the lands of north-west Wales. The old stories really do tell it like it was if you can read between their lines, they talk in analogies because we humans like that. Think about it, you remember and learn a lot from stories with characters you can really relate to, don't you? Those characters in our old stories were truly of the land, they had to be if they were to stand as mediators and teachers for us between the worlds of spirit and matter.

So ... those of us who are wledig, pagan, are deeply entwined with the land, plants, animals, wildlife, and the environment and how all that affects our gardens. That's what we're going

3

to explore in the rest of this book ... how getting connected can really help us all get the best from our gardening and from the whole of life too.

What's different about pagan gardening?

A modern term in western society nowadays is *mindfulness*, it helps people get away from the me-me-me-ness of modern life. While we who follow the old ways don't so much use the word *mindful* – we call it being present – it does really come to the same thing, close to describing the way we feel about everything; how we care about everything from the fridge to the forest, from the cow to the carrot to the computer. For us, there are no inanimate objects, everything, for us, has anima, spirit, soul, even the car and the computer. And the garden.

As we're people of the land we're often deeply involved in the environment and ecology, habitats, nature and the living landscape. We also have a deep connection with our gardens and all the creatures and plants there with whom we share it. We enjoy having wildlife around us and don't really use words like "pests" or "vermin". We know all life has a purpose and that Mother Earth didn't make any mistakes (except possibly with us!), so we work to understand what that purpose is. If that so-called weed is growing there why is that, what makes it happen, and so what do we need to be doing if there really is an imbalance.

In the old ways, we certainly garden organically, and to help wildlife, even if it's only in our window box or allotment. We don't use chemicals or GMO Roundup-Ready or other frightful stuff, and we don't do GMO seeds, most of us don't even do F1 hybrids. We do use most of the other ordinary gardening techniques like some digging, but many of us do as much permaculture and no-dig as we can. We make our own compost, save seeds, and encourage the mycorrhiza, and we often grow and harvest our own vegetables, fruit and flowers.

We do our best to grow what the land we're living with wants to grow, work-with it so things grow easily rather than needing to be forced into growth or supported by chemicals. The land grows what the land knows it wants to grow.

Sentient Plants

It's all about connections and consciousness ... but it isn't hard work, far from it! One of the things about being pagan is that you allow, know-in-your-bones even, that everything is sentient, conscious, aware, knowing itself and knowing self-from-other, they communicate with each other and other plants, feel pain and discomfort and fight against that too. They can solve problems, memorise things and learn, and they have their social life too.

One of the recent scientific researchers into all this is plant neurobiologist Stefano Mancuso, who works the University of Florence. His laboratory is becoming a place where plants are respected for their awareness and intelligence. He shows us that plants are able to solve problems, that they memorise, communicate, have their social life, and all the things we considered to be the province of humans, and maybe some animals. I hope his work will help us learn how to be a better species by observing the behaviour of our fellow living things with whom we share Planet Earth ... that's what we aim at in the old ways, learning how to be a better-quality human.

Mancuso says, *"When you feel yourself better than all the other humans or other living organisms, you start to use them. This is exactly what we've been doing. We felt ourselves as outside nature."* He points out that the typical lifespan of a species on Earth is between 2m and 5m years. *"Homo sapiens have lived just 300,000 years,"* he says, *"we have been able to almost destroy our environment. From this point of view, how can we say that we are better organisms?"* Definitely a thought to ponder.

Me ... or The Land?

Long ago and far away (as Star Wars says) I used to be a garden designer. I trained at Pershore College in Worcestershire in Britain, and my bragging rights include designing and building three medal-winning gardens at the Royal Horticultural Society's Hampton Court Palace garden show. It was fun ... and exhausting! I no longer design gardens except for myself but it did give me a lot of perspective on how people in general garden, what they want, what makes them happy, what various feel-good factors are. Unfortunately, many of the latter can be horrendously harmful for wildlife and the environment so, after three years, I walked away from garden design as I couldn't bear trying to force gardens into being what they really didn't want and couldn't handle. Reshaping the natural to suit human wants, is what has brought us into the perils of climate change.

Consciousness ...

OK, let's look at apple trees, did you know they can count? Peter Wohlleben in *The Hidden Life of Trees* has done lots of research for many years in Germany and shows that trees really can count! He discovered this from observation and found that trees count up a certain number of warm days and, when a certain number is reached, they trust it really is spring and open up their buds. Beech trees, for instance, don't start growing until it's light for at least thirteen hours a day. Scientists and gardeners found this out when observation showed them that the trees will not bloom, produce flowers, until there have been twenty frost-free days.

Do you see what this means? Trees are able to sense light, and even the quality of the light, *and* they can make sense of what they see to use it to regulate their own growth. Wow! That's huge. That says so much about plants that we've not known or believed for hundreds and probably thousands of years! Wohlleben's book has opened up the door for us again.

When we know this about plants it completely changes our

way of thinking about them and working with them. Most people think plants are inferior to themselves, as Mancuso says. But what happens when we begin to know and believe what he and Wohlleben tell us?

As pagans, we look at things differently and much nearer to what Wohlleben and Mancuso show and tell us, we know all things are animate, all things have spirit and soul.

When you know that about something or someone it's much harder to "use" them, or to abuse them. Spend a moment now thinking about that …

How does it make you feel about cutting down forests for windfarms or to drill for oil, for instance? Now try taking that a bit further, how does it feel to cut down forests – with all the creatures who live in them – to grow the wheat for your daily bread?

Difficult questions, aren't they? But they're ones that we worry and care about all the time as followers of the old pagan ways. I don't profess to have answers, but not having answers doesn't make me push the questions away, they still need thinking about especially in relation to how I live my life.

Seasons & Astronomy

Seasons

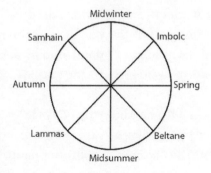

This diagram gives you the seasons of the year we pagans follow. Four of them you'll recognise – midwinter, spring, midsummer and autumn – the other four may be less familiar. This book is organised around the eight seasons so as you read it, you'll learn more about each, including the unfamiliar ones.

In the Northern Hemisphere, north is to the left. The Sun rises in the east, is at its highest in the *south*, then moves to the *right*, and sets in the west. Both rise and set positions move *northwards* from spring equinox to midsummer and then *southwards* from autumn equinox to midwinter.

In the Southern Hemisphere, south is to the left. The Sun rises in the east, is at its highest in the *north*, then moves to the *left*, to set in the west. Both rise and set positions move *southwards* from spring equinox (21st September) to midsummer (21st June) and *northwards* from autumn equinox (21st March) to midwinter (21st June).

The Earth and the Sun know where they are, all we humans need to do is follow their paths.

At the end of December (in the northern hemisphere) we see the Sun rise in the south-east to set in the south-west, describing a smallish arc in the sky (at noon, the Sun is fairly low on the horizon). But the following days, all the way to the end of June, it will rise a bit further north every day all the way to the north-east and similarly set further north-west, describing a much larger arc in the sky (at noon the Sun reaches the Zenith). We see the sun rise higher during the first half of the year and then lower in the second half of the year. The Moon has exactly the same course but its cycle last 27 days, 7 hours and 43 minutes.

The YEARLY sun-cycle gives us the seasons.

The Earth's yearly cycle

From midsummer to midwinter, the sun rises lower and lower each day, it sinks to its lowest point, its nadir, at midwinter. Then the cycle changes, swaps around. From midwinter to midsummer the sun rises higher and higher each day, until it's at its zenith at midsummer. Then it swaps back again. the cycles come turn-and-turn-about, year after year.

Half way between those two extreme points are the two equinoxes. The word equinox mean equal night, it's the day when there is an equal length of dark and light for that one day. The equinoxes happen each spring and autumn, they're part of the Earth/Sun's yearly cycle.

So, the sun offers the experience of both extremes, and the experience of balance.

While the Earth is "breathing out", from midwinter to midsummer, she is also pushing the energy up through the roots into the parts of the plant above the ground – leaves, flowers and fruit.

This breathing process is part of what sets seeds off to germinate and why germination is much stronger during spring and up to midsummer, because there's more and more light.

A brief jaunt into a bit of astronomy will help explain so much of what goes on in our gardens.

Astronomically, in our solar system, midwinter truly is the turning of the year. At the autumn equinox the sun rises due east and sets due west, the equinoxes are the only times this happens. After the equinox the sun rises further and further south of east and the sun rises in the south-east, while it sets further and further south-west – thus the daylight hours become shorter and shorter. Until we come to midwinter, then the sun turns around.

As part of its turning around it seems to pause for three days and rise at the same place on the horizon, this happens on 22nd, 23rd and 24th of December. On the 25th the sun turns eastward again, rising each day a little further north of south east until it get to spring equinox when it rises due east again. All this time the sun has also be setting a little further north each day too, so the daylight hours get longer and longer each day.

Then from spring equinox to midsummer, the sun rises and

sets further and further north each day. The daylight hours get longer and we enjoy the summer. At midsummer, the sun turns around again, pausing for three days as it does so and, again appearing to rise at the same point on the horizon for the 22nd, 23rd and 24th of June, moving on again to rise and set further south each day.

And so, the cycle continues, year in and year out for the past 4.7-ish billion years at the latest guess. Of course, our ancient ancestors noticed this phenomenon (along with all the rest of the movements of the heavens); they lived so much closer and more connectedly with the Earth, and the heavens too, than we do nowadays. And being connected they likely felt as we pagans do, that we and the rest of the universe are made of the same stuff even if it comes out in all different shapes and sizes – mountains, rivers, sea, animals, birds, rocks. And that's true, we are indeed all made of the same atoms and those same atoms cycle around, sometimes being a human, sometimes a cabbage, sometimes a cat! Our ancestors likely knew, as we pagans do, that everything in creation is our brother and our elder too as humans are the most recent species on Planet Earth so everything else is older than us. As pagans, we try to learn from our elders ... and that includes gardening!

Midwinter Solstice

Season

Midwinter solstice is the time of the shortest day.
Solstice means standstill.
3 days of standstill.

Midwinter is about the turnaround of the sun. That's literal too, that's what actually happens astronomically in the heavens, it's not just a pagan idea; our practices really are based in what happens in fact in the Solar System, and in the whole galaxy. Our ancient ancestors knew and understood this even if they maybe didn't have our modern scientific language, what we call physics, to explain it; and part of knowing – we call it kenning from the old northern verb to ken meaning to know, like in the song "D'ye Ken John Peel" – is knowing what's going on with the whole plant kingdom. The plants help us understand the real turning of the seasons. To be a successful hunter-gatherer you have to know what's happening in the forests, valleys, rivers, mountains, open plains and in the sea too. You won't have a clue where to look for things to eat, what animals are doing what and when, if you don't understand how the whole system works. We've lost a lot of that over the past 10,000 years, but gardening can reconnect us with all of that, yes, really, all of it.

Element

Stone, soil, rocks ... all the things that are the skeleton of Mother Earth.

The Stone People are special to me, archaeologists call that time the Paleolithic. Paleo comes from the Greek word *palaios*, meaning old, and the Greek word *lithos* meaning stone, so it means the Old Stone Age. It was followed by the Meso or Middle Stone Age and then a couple of thousand years later by the

Neolithic or New Stone Age which ended very roughly about 6,500 years ago as we emerged into the Copper, Bronze and Iron ages. What we call modern history is just a mere 2000 years old.

As Homo Sapiens evolved around 300,000 years ago almost all of our history has been in the Stone Ages, only the past 6,500 years have we been metal people, so the Stone People are my ancestors and completely fascinating to me.

Altar

You'll not be surprised that we make and use and keep altars as pagans. Actually, lots of folk do this, have a special place where they put special things that remind them of what's important to them. And we all collect pebbles and stones, maybe crystals too, they can be so attractive as you walk along the beach or over the hillside.

We also make our altars in the direction that corresponds to the season we're working with. Midwinter holds the energy of the North, the place of darkness in the northern hemisphere. If you're working in the southern hemisphere just turn it upside-down, in the southern half of the world the place of darkness is the South Pole.

My altar for Midwinter is always about Stone, the stone-people, the mineral kingdom; they remind me, make me remember, the crazy spinning rock on which we live. If our 3rd Rock from the Sun wasn't here, careering round the Sun at about 70,000 mph, we wouldn't have anywhere to live; and if the Earth in her turn wasn't spinning round on her axis at roughly 1,000 mph, we wouldn't live either. It sounds completely nuts when you try to think about it but it feels right and real, just how it should be.

So, I build my Midwinter Altar with all that in mind. It has whichever of the special rocks in my collection want to be there this time, and they always include at least one hag stone. Hag stones are so special to pagans, stones with holes worn in them by the action of water and sometimes wind. They're also called holey stones for that hole, it's like a gateway or threshold to another place or between worlds. That reminds me that we're always living on the edge, between past and future ... living in the Now.

I build my Midwinter altar to the Stone People who certainly (from their fantastic art) knew how to live in the Now.

Plants

Are totally amazing beings. They're far, far older than humans and have been living with the Earth for at least 500 million years ... that 500,000,000, a helluva a lot of zeros! They're much more experienced at living with the Earth than I and other humans are so I watch and learn from them as much as I can. There's nothing like learning from those who have far more experience than yourself.

One of the amazing (to us modern humans) things plants can do is count day-lengths, for instance since the last frost. They need this ability to know day-length, know the waxing and waning of sunlight and temperature, to help them know when to let a seed fall, or begin to sprout, when to produce their flowers, when to turn their flowers into seeds, and when to drop their leaves, or go back down into the ground for the winter.

That's awesome when you think about it. Even as a lifelong gardener I'm not that good. I can get close but not with the accuracy of a tree or a plant. And I have to think and worry at it, scribble notes, look things up, do maths, while plants know how to do it in their bones ... or perhaps I should say cells as they sure don't have bones!

They know all these changes through their sensitivity to both light and temperature. They're able to work out how many times the sun has risen since the last frost. Wow!

Trees and plants do other amazing things too. They can actually count! I know it sounds amazing but trees will count the last frost to begin putting out their flower buds. They've actually been doing this for some 3,500-million years. Phew! That's a long time, you can understand they've developed some experience at doing this by now. That's when photosynthesis began in simple single-celled algae, and from that beginning comes all the wonderful variety of plants we see today; I call that pretty hot work for Planet Earth.

The first land plants appeared around 470 million years ago, during the Ordovician period, when life was diversifying rapidly.

Herbs

As well as the Old Wives in the village I've learned a lot from Scottish friends about their folk herb traditions.

Midwinter feels like being "in the darkness", indeed it is the time of the greatest darkness, the shortest day, the winter solstice, when the sun reaches the lowest arc in the sky before turning about and beginning a rising arc again. For us it's often the end of January before we really notice the light increasing again. The sun rises late and sets early. On clear days, the beautiful crimson-orange light of dawn and dusk spreads through the landscape, highlights the bare stark trees. It's a time for turning inwards, reviewing the past year and sorting ideas for the coming one, and for the garden too.

Within ourselves and within the garden it's a natural time for dormancy and retreat, but our modern life doesn't allow for that, we can feel pressured into *bravehearting* our way through this time, that we must keep pushing, working and achieving. The midwinter holidays often bring a rise in emotional, financial and physical stress, and SAD (seasonal affective disorder) can strike to make us feel miserable and low in energy. That's hard. And it's not Nature's way – our modern life runs against nature so often but as pagans we work to not allow this to happen too much while still being a part of the 21st century.

So how do pagans work with this? One way is to join in with the natural world, to feel and watch that beautiful midwinter glow allowing it to fill our hearts. When we do that it changes our hormones from stress towards joy, eases tension, encourages blood-flow that helps warm our bodies, brightens our day.

We also look to our native plants for help. There are remedies to help catch the sun's rays and its warm feeling, herbs for acceptance of where we are in the natural cycle that hold and gift us this feeling. They support us through this time of year, as other herbs do at other times. Our ancestors knew this well; I remember the older folk – those who followed the old ways – in the village where I grew up showing us children how to work with them.

Veg

For Midwinter we usually think of roots – beautifully roasted potatoes, carrots glazed in honey, deep fried parsnips. Our Palaeolithic ancestors knew about the benefits of fat and how it actually feeds the brain, they ate roots too and our modern root veg come from these. They ate lots of green leaves and there are lots of leaves available at midwinter, especially from the brassica family. If you grow brassicas – cabbages, kale, Brussels sprouts, cauliflower, purple sprouting and such – you know how well they stand throughout the worst of winters. Leeks too will stand through all seasons so there's lots of leaves available, especially if you've been able to grow them yourself.

I love to pick fresh. I go out into the garden and literally call out to the plants, "Hey guys, what are you giving me for my dinner today?" and I can feel which ones to go for. Sounds crazy I know in our modern world! I take students out doing this too when they're here for a long weekend workshop and by day two they've got the hang of it even if they've never done it before in their lives. Do try it for yourself, perhaps with nobody else around at first in case you feel embarrassed, trust yourself, trust your knowing, it's an inbuilt feature for all humans if we'll only allow it.

After that scrumptious meal how about sitting down with a pad and pen, by the fire with that after dinner cuppa, and making a list of the vegetables you really enjoy eating? You could plan to grow them next year, maybe this year's growing list needs a bit of adaptation as your tastes may have changed, mine do now and again. If you're not sure how to grow some of them then Google them, there's lots of good growing advice on the web, organic and permaculture advice too.

The veg beds at this time of year are partially dormant but your winter salads will hopefully be thriving as well as your brassicas, onions, beetroots and such. We suffer badly from winds up here at 500ft, 40mph quite often and gusts well above that. Wind can damage plants and not just by blowing them over. We all hear of wind-chill from the weather-people on TV and that affects plants just as badly as us, worse in fact as we can go indoors and get warm but the plants can't. Wind-break shelter is really necessary and the best of all is thick, well-cared for native hedging; I'm lucky, I live out in the country and have a lot of that, if you don't there are other ways.

It's good to know a bit about how wind works if you're a gardener. Being pagan helps too as you're already very interested in the natural world and how it works. So how does nature do it, organise shelter from the winds?

Hedges work because they don't "stop" the wind but "filter" it. Moving air does get through but because it's had to fight its way through a tangle of branches and leaves it's lost 80 or even 90 per cent of its energy. So, what was a 40mph wind one side of the hedge is barely a 5 or 10mph wind by the time it gets through and as it's going much more slowly it's also lost its wind-chill factor. It doesn't hurt the plants any more, in fact that gently moving air really helps to lift frost and stir up any fungal growth that was hoping to latch onto your plants.

Thick copses of trees work in a similar way as long as they have plenty of "understorey" amongst them, if they don't then the lower level wind nearer the ground is still whizzing along at 40mph and will cause damage. So, if you have a copse by your garden for all the gods' sakes don't "tidy it up" or you'll cause one helluva lot of damage to your garden as well as depriving insects, birds and small mammals of their natural habitat ... and so helping to cause extinctions!

But if you don't live in a place where you can have a hedge, or a copse, what can you do? There's some excellent wind-break netting available in garden centres and online, this really does do the job and in a similar way to hedges in that its small holes filter the wind. Do use it if you have any kind of wind problem. Another way is fencing but ... but ... do be careful what fencing you get! Most of the popular fencing readily available, and reasonably cheap, is as much use as an ashtray on a motorbike (to quote my husband, Paul!) because it blocks, stops the wind. Well you actually can't stop wind, it won't let you, and its much bigger and more powerful than any human or group of humans. If you put a block in the way of the wind it goes round and/or over. And the block actually causes it to speed up, just to make things worse.

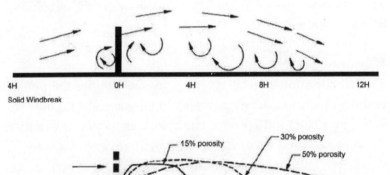

4H   0H   4H   8H   12H
Solid Windbreak

15% porosity   30% porosity   50% porosity

4H   0H   4H   8H   12H
Porous Windbreak

These diagrams show the difference in air-flow between a solid wall (top) and a porous, hedge-like fence. Do you see how the wind dives and swirls behind the solid wall? Imagine that. Better still go find one on a windy day and stand there, feel it … it's not pleasant. If you put up the usual solid fence around your garden you create this turbulence behind your fence for your plants to suffer – not a good idea.

But you can get porous fencing, like wattle and willow hurdles, and this works just fine. There's also cheaper machine-made porous fencing if you look around a bit at garden centres and online. Because neither of these are solid, they filter the wind and slow it down in a similar way to the hedge.

Look at something else in the bottom diagram too. Do you see how the wind shelter ability of the fence increases with its porosity? The 15% porous only shelter a short way from the fence whereas the 50% porosity shelters over 3 times as far. Nature does this out in the wild, very clever as she always is once we look and observe what and how she does things. As always, it's really a good idea to copy her ways.

And another point about hedges and careful natural style fences is they can become habitat for insects, butterflies, bees, birds and small mammals … if you don't weed them to within an inch of their lives. We'll talk more about this in the Imbolc and Spring chapters.

Flowers

Flowers for midwinter … oh there are lots besides the potted, hothouse plants all the shops offer you for your celebrations. The Woodland Trust and Trees for Life, two of my favourite charities, are very good and informative about our native wildflowers.

Winter jasmine and winter honeysuckle are two of my favourites because they both scent up the air so deliciously. They're both climbers so good for wall and arches but they also do well as hedging plants, giving a good thick tangle of stems and branches that is also excellent habitat for all those wee beasties we rely on for pollination as well as winter shelter for birds and mammals. If you have acid soil then you can enjoy witch-hazel, daphne, camellias and heathers too. Garrya elliptica, the Silk Tassel Bush, is an amazing plant with huge great long slender dangles of pale cream tassels of flowers that are 20cm long. They shine out from amongst the glossy, wavy-edged, dark green leaves throughout winter, from December to February and provide pollen for any bees or butterflies who've woken out of winter hibernation. It's great towards the back of a sunny shrub border, or against a wall, and makes a great windbreak habitat too. When it's done flowering the dark foliage makes a lovely background for summer flowers. Mahonia is another gorgeous architectural shrub with fabulously scented golden flower stalks though November to March. It's tall and spikey, if you want to keep people out of your garden it does a grand job at this too. All the viburnums have lovely scented flowers too and are excellent shrub-hedge habitat makers, and so are all the winter box, the Sarcococca family, and they're scented as well.

Hellebores, also known as Christmas roses, are a stalwart in my garden. They're so beautiful and again keep going, producing their beautiful white flowers throughout the midwinter season. I love Helleborus purpurascens, the pinky-purple one as well as the stunning white Helleborus niger. We'll talk about their pink and purple sisters for Imbolc and Spring too.

I have a passion for Cyclamen coum too. The country name for them is *sowbread*, I don't know why. I love the way their delicate pink flowers, with the upswept petals, appear in above rounded, silvery-green leaves and they naturalise beautifully around the base of deciduous trees and shrubs. They like to be in partial shade and make excellent companions for ferns in the little woodland corner I call The Wolery – that's Owl's House from Winnie the Pooh.

There's also Bergenia, also known as Elephant's Ears from its big round leaves that send up spikes of pink or white flowers from January to April. And Iris unguicularis, the Algerian winter iris that flowers from October to March; it's a vigorous evergreen perennial with lots of dark green leaves and very fragrant, deep violet flowers that are marked with white and deep yellow at the base in late winter. Quite stunning.

Garden Jobs

Soil – the element of earth

Soil is made from the rocks that are the bones of Mother Earth. Soil is a living and dynamic ecosystem. The spaces in between soil particles allow water and nutrients to pass through them, those spaces also preserve and hold that water and those nutrients. The spaces between have a dual role and one that seems opposite at first glance – they *both* hold and pass water and nutrients. Pagan craft tells us the natural world – including the whole universe – is inclusive, works on the and/and principle not the either/or. And that certainly goes for gardening.

As I said, soil is fascinating stuff, all different shapes and sizes because of the rock it's made from. Clay gets a really bad press still with lots of gardeners but maybe they don't realise just how fantastic the stuff is. Clay is made of extremely fine particles, that's part of the problem with it sticking together so well we find it hard to dig and it can dry out like concrete. But those ultra-fine particles hold water so much more readily than the larger particles of, say, sand. I'm sure you know the amount of available water in your soil has profound consequences for your garden. Like us, plants die of thirst and they will die much more readily if your soil can't hold the water for them very well. And water does other things too, like help balance soil surface temperatures and regulate how hot the soil can get; in its turn, that affects seed germination, flowering and fruiting.

Dung (what we often call Muck), is a major key to good soil health. The best muck comes from cows as they give the largest quantity of muck and they're ruminants. Ruminants are beasties who have 4 stomachs, so their digestive system is very long and very thorough. The 4 stomachs remind me of the four processes of alchemy:

Nigredo – when we put the kitchen caddy, lawn mowings, weeds and the fresh dung into the compost heap.
Albedo – when the heap is working, the bugs and worms transforming what was waste into the next stage of producing soil.
Citrinato – when the compost sits "proving" rather like bread, a waiting time while it becomes good soil again.
Rubado – when it's soil, full of goodness and life and nutrients that are ready to be taken up by the plants again to help them grow.

So, the food the cow eats goes through an alchemical process in her gut to come out the other end as really magical stuff helping your soil become really healthy.

But organic matter can be more than cow muck, in fact it's *anything* that contains carbon; that's anything that was ever a living organism – lawn mowings, leaves, stems, branches, kitchen waste, plants-in-the-wrong-place (weeds!), moss algae, lichens, old pond weed, sawdust and chipped tree-brash. The insects, earthworms and microbes will do their magic on all of that and give us good soil again. It's the contents of your compost bin, and you collect all that and give it back to your garden in exchange for all the flowers and veg and fruit you enjoy through the year.

What you want/need to grow in your garden makes a big difference to the sort of soil it requires to do that for you. Our native plants are well adapted to our natural soils, but there's no point in trying to grow meadowsweet in a dry summer meadow when what it needs is a nice damp ditch. You do have to notice and observe how nature does it and then emulate that if you can, so think about where the plants grow in the wild and give them similar conditions in your garden.

But don't try to push your garden into being what it wasn't made to do. You can't turn an alkali soil into an acid one, don't care what all the garden centres and books tell you, it won't happen without you continually and expensively keep giving the soil acid-making substances like sphagnum peat (horribly bad for the environment!), elemental sulphur, aluminium sulphate, iron sulphate, acidifying nitrogen, and others. You effectively have to feed what is poison to your soil to try to make it happen but ... your garden will stop it, change its soil back to how the rocks from which it comes want it to be. So, you keep buying more stuff ... while the garden gets cross and turns all your efforts back on themselves.

Using your organic mulches of compost and muck will move the soil pH closer to the mean half way mark between acid and alkali, and that will stick, your garden will like that, but it won't make it possible for you to grow camellia and rhodos in your alkali garden!

Vegetables are not natural, native plants although they've all been bred from natural plants to begin with. The breeding has changed them radically from the original wild plants. Carrots for instance were little tiny yellowish roots with great tall stems climbing out of the grass covered with umbels of lacy white flowers. Beautiful but you probably wouldn't enjoy them much. I'm a bit of a wild forager too so I've tried them. A word of warning – the wild carrot family includes the deadly poisonous hemlock and hemlock water-dropwort so please don't go foraging unless you really know your plants or are with someone who does!

So, our modern vegetables need a much richer loamy soil that holds water without water logging, and allows air into the soil so that roots and soil organisms can thrive.

Such a soil will be high in organic matter too, as that gives lots of porous space for the water and nutrients to flow through. It can also hold the water and nutrients in like reserve storage to be released as the plants require them. If there's the right amount of muck and compost going into it, you'll find the soil has a neutral or slightly acidic pH as that's just the champagne veggies enjoy.

It's worth remembering our modern vegetables are very tough on the soil, they take loads of food, loads more than their wild ancestors needed, can be tender and far more prone to disease. They have lots of needs and are high-maintenance. But they do taste marvellous, and home-grown organic veg are bung full of goodness so it's well worth the effort.

One of the reasons they're hard on the soil is because we don't let them die back and give the goodness they've taken out of the soil back to it. We eat them, so their goodness goes into us instead and not back into the soil. This means we must give something back to the soil in return or it just can't keep producing for us, hence composting and finding a regular source of good cow muck. We need to replenish the soil if we're going to ask Mother Earth to keep feeding us and the best thing we can give back to her are the carbon beings she made in the first place.

Something I find good to remember is that for all of her 4.5 billion years of life, Earth has cycled and recycled every single atom of herself, round and round they go one time a cabbage, next a horse, maybe a human, then a lion … round and round we go. As the old adage says, what goes around comes around, and that's a very good one to remember for us gardeners. Perhaps instead of straining our brains to think up new ways to replenish her, like new manmade chemicals, in the manner of teenagers, who always know best how to rule the world, we do much better to watch and notice and copy her ways, they've worked very well without our manmade chemicals for most of that 4.5 billion years. Let's give her lots of muck and compost in thanks for the food she gives us.

Roots: What's happening with the Plants at Midwinter

Winter is a really important time for plants and the soil. As pagan gardeners, we work very closely with the soil and the whole plant kingdom and find it really helps our gardens.

Over winter plants tend to shut down, even evergreen ones. Herbaceous plants lose all their foliage, they do this by cutting off the sap-flow as autumn progresses and we see this most spectacularly as the leaves turn colour giving us their wonderful fiery display. The leaves drop and are reabsorbed into the soil – giving back and exchange again – so their goodness can be taken up into the trees in the coming year. So, we don't burn the leaves that fall in our gardens, we make leaf mould and add them to the compost so they can feed the trees and plants again next year. Many of us don't sweep up the leaves unless we need to either; I prefer they don't lie about in my wildflower meadows as they'll enrich the soil too much and make it inedible to the wildflowers so I use those for give-back stuff like compost and leaf mould. But in the woodland part of the garden, the Wolery, I let them lie under the hedges to feed the hedgerow plants and the tree and bushes that make the hedges themselves. I don't feel the need to do it for Mother Nature but let her get on with it in her own way.

The roots of herbaceous plants spend the winter drinking water and nourishment, feeding and caring for themselves with the help of the *mycorrhizae* – that's the amazing fungus that could (and should) spread all across the surface of Planet Earth. This habit of root nourishment is one reason why we prefer to plant trees and roses between November and March, it give their roots the chance to bed themselves in, get firmly attached to the life-giving fungus and so well nourished before they feel the need to spend energy producing leaves, flowers and fruit. Trees that have been well bedded-in over winter will come into their spring growth season much better able to do their stuff. So, don't go thinking the plants are all asleep over the winter, they're working hard underground, preparing for the coming spring.

Plants – indeed all of wild nature – is completely in tune with the movements of the sun. They know, their sensory abilities are that good, how much light comes from the sun each day. They sense the shortest day and the three-day standstill; science has discovered how accurately their timing works. Second by second, minute by minute, and day by day they know exactly how much light there is each day and adjust their growth accordingly, they call this the *circadian rhythm*, and we humans have this too only we've stopped being aware of it unless we take the trouble to relearn it. Everything on Earth has this rhythm and everything but we humans work naturally and instinctively with it – we need to relearn and gardening helps us do that. Humans mostly live detached from nature, in our cities with continuous artificial light so we've lost the ability to sense the natural rhythm of everything. But plants still have all their senses intact and they use them, they sense the signals that come from the changing light and so, as winter progresses towards spring, they change their underground workings towards the process of growing leaves again.

A pagan way of life is usually fairly well in tune with the natural seasons so pagan gardeners work naturally with the plants and their senses. Our rituals and practices help us to be more in tune with the natural world and less disconnected.

New year for plants, especially herbaceous plants, means the change from being dormant to beginning the process of awakening again and occurs on the solstice time as they sense the changing arc of the sun. Their awakening starts then, and so the process of growing leaves, then flowers and finally fruits again begins far underground, in the womb of the soil. As pagan gardeners, because we know the process of the midwinter solstice from our own craft, and so we help the plants with their process as they help us with ours.

Midwinter & Celebration

For many pagans all around the world the beginning of the year is the midwinter solstice. It's the shortest day, 21st Dec ... from now on until Midsummer, the days get longer and longer. It's the rebirth of the Sun.

It's also the time of Stone. Stone is the bones of Mother Earth. As they say in the TV sitcom, we live on the Third Rock from the Sun. And stone, rock, geology, is vital for gardening – we wouldn't have any soil without it.

Celebrating Midwinter

We begin to celebrate on 20th Dec, Midwinter's Eve, and our celebration often goes on until 12th Night, the 6th January. For us, it's a sun-time, a time that comes under the aegis of the sun. Our Stone Age ancestors knew this as we can see from monuments like Stonehenge that celebrate the winter solstice. Plants know it's new year too, whether they're evergreen like holly or herbaceous, and the way they grow begins to change after the winter solstice. Our ancient ancestors knew-in-their-bones that this is the turn-of-the-year, and we can know this again too, for ourselves, through our gardens.

The time between Midwinter and Imbolc (31st January) often seems dark, bare, cold and depressing for us humans and that's partly because we don't remember what's happening underground. Like I said, the herbaceous plants – plants that lose their leaves and disappear back into the earth over the winter – are big gamechangers for us because they reappear at the end of winter. But I'm getting ahead of myself, more on that time in the next chapter, for now let's stay with winter.

Once the sun has turned around the Earth responds. All the plants begin to stir again, the birds sing more and begin mating and so do the animals. We humans are often so disconnected now from the cycles of Earth and Sun we don't feel it as our ancestors did. But if you go out now, at the beginning of solstice and smell the soil then, after the solstice go out and sniff the soil again ... well ... can you smell the difference? Many people can.

Go out in your garden every season and feel, sense, how it changes, listen to the birds, watch the plants and flowers and trees. Enjoy the awakening and changing of the Earth.

Meditation – Standstill Ruminations

So just what is going on at midwinter, and what do pagans do to get involved with those changes, and to be useful to Mother Earth?

Something I do every Midwinter is go back over the past year, making a two-column list of the happenings of the past year, what felt good, what felt difficult and uncomfortable in some way, and then I use the three days of the standstill for reflection on all those events. Not just garden happenings either but all the events of the past year. As a pagan I live in an *and/and* universe and know myself to be connected with everything, so I know that the car breakdown had knock-on effects to my gardening and all my home and work life too. The new cat who came to live with me has changed everything in my life too. Things like a friend's daughter's new boyfriend changes relationships, as does that their son got straight 'A's in all his exams, that another friend got poorly and nearly died, that a branch broke off a tree and squashed some plants. All these things affect every aspect of our lives, life really is connected ... we just need to remember to join up all the dots!

The word *solstice* means to standstill. It refers to the effect we notice that for the three days after the solstice (either winter or summer solstice) the sun appears to rise at the same point on the horizon for three days. Of course, our ancestors noticed this too as their lives were much more deeply involved with the natural world and the seasons than ours are. That's one of the reasons why Stonehenge is aligned as it is, not just that the midsummer sun rises over the heel-stone but also that the midwinter sun sets between the two great standing stones that are connected by the stone lintel over the top. Archaeology has discovered the enormous remains of our feasting on these occasions too, so we certainly knew the phenomenon and celebrated it.

Many of us pagans still use those three days to ponder and ruminate and muse on the events of the past year to see what we can learn from them, how we might change things, do things differently. We celebrate the joys of the past year and we grieve the losses too – grief is really important and not to be thrust away pretending it didn't happen. Even the loss of those lettuces to the slugs needs grieving! It also needs us to ponder on how (other than slug pellets) we might save enough lettuces for ourselves in the coming year. A good way to do that is to learn about slugs, what they do, why and how. If we remove the root cause of why the slugs ate our lettuces then we properly eliminate the problem, not just put Band-Aid over the wound.

So, your three days contemplation could well include learning about all the beasties you share your garden with. How do hedgehogs and ducks work with slugs? What about thrushes and snails? Ladybirds and greenfly? Did you know those fantastically beautiful dragonflies eat midges? Maybe killing the midges also starves the dragonflies? Hmmm … lots to ponder over in the dark, cosy evening by the log fire at midwinter.

Meditation – Standstill Contemplation
This is a little exercise I always do over Midwinter. I find it really useful and it allows and enables some me-time on what's often the busiest time of the year for families.

Try to do this on 21st Dec, Midwinter's Day.

Find a bridge over a stream or river.

Face down stream, compose yourself and say "*I let go of everything in my life that's past its sell-by date. I thank it for bringing me to the here and now. I let it go to flow back into the great stream of everything so it can be useful for others.*" Stand for a moment, feeling it all flow out of you.

Now, turn to face upstream, compose yourself, say, "*I open myself to the future. I am willing to receive all that otherworld has for me. Help me to walk the next step on my journey to learn to be useful to Mother Earth.*" Stand for a moment, feeling it all flow into you.

Thank the bridge for being there and helping you with this ritual. Pull your thought-threads in, don't leave thoughts and emotional clutter for the next person who comes to the bridge, nor for the bridge itself. Let go of everything and go home.

Back home, get yourself a cuppa and a piece of cake, sit down somewhere quiet and make yourself a two-column list. Head one column "Joys" and the other "Sorrows". Then, over the time it takes to enjoy your tea-n-cake, begin making a list of the things that came to mind at the bridge.

But don't stop there, over the three days of standstill, that's the 22nd, 23rd and 24th Dec, keep adding to the list. Each day, sit-with ideas that come up from your list so far, ruminate (remember ruminants and alchemy?) and contemplate with them, see what other ideas they bring up and note those down too. I always do this over a cup of tea or coffee depending on what time of day I do my sit-with, we pagans do believe in enjoyment!

Then, on 25th Dec when the sun moves on again (we pagans call it Sun Return), I make time amongst all the cooking and eating of the celebration dinner to be quiet and alone for half an hour. It's a really good idea as the celebrations can make one feel quite frazzled. I take a glass of wine with me, all my notes from the three days of the standstill and a pen, put a "Do not disturb!" notice on my door and have another sit-with, with all that's come up.

For me this always includes things that have happened in the garden, like how early the roses bloomed, how two months of no rain nearly lost me my apples, how to do fruit tree watering better, which lettuce varieties I liked best, how well the potatoes stored, which hardy geraniums did best and how much seed I was able to collect. You're getting the idea. The pondering also takes in how home and work crises (there are always some, aren't there?) affected the garden as well as how they frustrated me. And I'm always allowing ideas to come up for how to do things better – and jotting them down so I don't forget!

I find this really works well. I get perspective on the past year and so am able to see new ways of doing things, and new things to do as well, much more easily. Sitting quiet, with a cuppa or a glass of wine, relaxed, not pushing or struggling for answers, I'm able to just let the thoughts come trickling into my mind. Often, they come as pictures so I doodle them, not just using words; they're no works of art but the doodle-scribbles are good reminders of the ideas. And I can fairly easily transpose them into garden plans.

Imbolc

Season

Imbolc is the first season we celebrate of each new *calendar year*, the everyday year that we all follow for our everyday lives. It's the threshold between winter and spring. It's no longer the depths of winter as it is at Midwinter but it's not yet Spring either.

Ceridwen, the Dark Crone, holds winter for us as I was brought up. She's the old one, the wise one who knows all the past and holds in her cauldron stirring it over the fire through the dark days. On the third day of the standstill it bubbles and boils and throws out its three drops of wisdom for the year and she catches them in her cup and holds them. When Imbolc comes, she passes the cup to Bridey, the Maid of Spring.

For us, it can signify the end of a long period of endurance, the end of the dark days of winter. Oh yes, the days began to get lighter from the 25th of December but it always seems hard to notice for the whole of January and can indeed feel like when is this ever going to end? We long to be free again feel the light and warmth on our skin.

We have stories for all the seasons, you can find many of them in the Story Cave on the Deer Trods Tribe website, and the Imbolc tale of Bridey's Snake is also there as a podcast. The Dark Crone and the Bright Spring Maid come together at the Well of Wisdom where the old one passes the cup to the young one for her to now hold the three drops of wisdom.

For me, I always feel it's time to turn over a new leaf, and I feel this in the garden too. The early plants are pushing out their first buds, beginning to count the frost-free days to judge when it's time to let their buds burst. I follow suit, watch the budding trees preparing to let go of the dark and heavy work of the womb they've carried all winter long; I watch the snowdrops birth themselves out of the dark cold earth. They bring the sense of newness into my life.

Element

As I'm sure you know there are only the four elements – earth, water, air and fire – in our European pagan calendar and those four are the elements we work with at the Sun-Seasons of Midwinter (earth/stone), Spring (water), Midsummer (air), and Autumn (fire). So, what elements do we work with at what's known as the cross-quarters of Imbolc, Beltane, Lammas and Samhain? Well my dad, relations and the old ones in the villages in Devon where I grew up used a combination of the two elements either side and called those seasons between places.

So, Imbolc is the between place of earth/stone and water. This always feels good to me, a sort of slithery place where the soil softens and the water changes from being nearer its solid state of ice and grows into its fluid state of water.

Altar & Focusing Ritual

Combinations of earth and water are the order of the day for me at my Imbolc altar and yes, I do actually include mud here! That's ordinary garden mud made by mixing a little bit of soil with a little water.

I take a spoonful of mud and three spoonsful of water and stir them together with my finger (see my ritual below). Being pagan really does mean you quickly get over the modern fears and taboos about "dirt", soil and water are part of the Mother's body so how can they possibly not be sacred?

If you fear there could be *nasties* in your soil, maybe you've not been there long and so don't know what the previous people used in their garden, or you may even have some stuff like old tin cans and broken bottles when you dug then you know to wash your hands well when you're done soap and water really does fix a lot of germ-stuff we don't need in our bodies as people discovered with the COVID-19 pandemic. I had the old tin cans still with bits of stuff in them and broken dirty bottles in my first year when I moved to Bryngwyn, the person before me was not very clean!

So, having got over any fear of dirt, you can mix the mud using garden soil and garden water. If you have a pond then definitely use this water, if you don't and your water has been chlorinated then allow it to stand in a jug for a few hours so the chlorine can evaporate. That's good for your drinking water too, I always leave a glass handy and evaporating so I have good water when I want it. And tell the water what you would like to use it for, we always respect and acknowledge the spirit (anima) in everything, it really helps you get connected with Mother Earth and the natural world.

Now … first, get your compass and find where the north-east corner of your garden is – north-east corresponds with Imbolc for us – this will be the place for your altar and ritual. Set up a stone, or a piece of wood, or a log, as your table.

Then, I make a triangle out of three willow twigs tied together with a piece of plaited (braided) wool of three colours – red, white and black. They're the three colours of Bridey and she's the patron goddess of Imbolc, and willow is her sacred tree. More about her at the end of this section.

Take a small bowl you're really fond of, tell the bowl that you would like to use it as the *cauldron* to make your magic Imbolc potion in and ask the bowl if that's OK with it. You'll almost certainly get a Yes but should it happen to be a No ask the bowl what you could use instead, you'll quickly know what container will be right.

Then get your spoonful of soil. Stand in the garden and ask, "Where's the soil I'm to use for my Imbolc altar, please?" You'll get drawn to a place and it will be easy to get the spoonful of soil, a few wee stones in it help as they remind you of the Stone People. Put it in your cauldron.

Add your three spoonsful of water. As you stir the soil and water together with your finger ask them both to combine into the magical potion you and the garden need for this Imbolc. I always stir three times anticlockwise (we call that widdershins) then three times clockwise (we call that deosil, pronounced *dash-ill*), and then three times widdershins again, so nine times in all.

When it's mixed, dab your muddy finger on your forehead and then on both cheeks. As you do this say, "One for Mother Earth, two for my spirit, three for my body." This little ritual helps affirm your connection with the Earth and the natural world again.

Leave the mud on your face as long as you can, it won't hurt. And leave the willow triangle on the stone in that north-east corner where you did your ritual, along with the bowl of mud. You pack it all away at the end of the season as you did for Midwinter.

Nine is a very magical number for most pagans; for me it reminds me of Bridey's nine fires that she and her human representatives, priestesses if you like, keep alive for us all throughout the year. The Christians have taken the idea of our nine fires and call this season Candlemas – so many of their rituals they've taken from us. They knew we old ones wouldn't stop our old ways easily, didn't want to convert, so they said if we can't stop these people celebrating in their old ways so we'll convert things a wee bit and tell them what they're really doing is our way … sigh!

You may know Bridey better as Bridget or Brighid but in the lands where I grew up and now live, we call her Bridey. We know her as the Lady (goddess) of the of the Three Faces – Blacksmith, Healer, Poet, and Maiden, Mother, Crone.

Plants
Plants that mean a lot to me at Imbolc

These plants always give me such a delight as we come out of the short dark winter days, when it stops getting dark at 4pm and when I can get up before 8am without needing to turn on all the lights.

- Snowdrops – Bridey's flower, and so for me *the flower* of the season, I always have them in my garden and bring some into the house as part of my Imbolc celebrations.
- Winter aconites
- Hellebores
- Winter Jasmine
- Crocus
- Wintersweet
- Witch Hazel
- Algerian iris – not a native but oh so beautiful, and scented
- Viburnum always smells so good as well as providing food for early bees
- Winter honeysuckle also has a lovely scent and is bee-provender

Veg

So, how about the veg garden? There are a few green things I like to grow that tide me over the dark Midwinter. Kale is always good and there are many ways to cook and use it too. It will stand over the winter out in the garden pretty well whatever the weather, and if you grow kale-tops in the window you can use them for cut-n-come-again fresh salad. Winter cabbage is another one that works in many dishes. If you have a polytunnel there's lots of salad you can keep coming too, it only needs frost protection.

And Imbolc is a good time to discuss with the garden what it, and you, would like to grow later in the year.

Plants I like to forage at this time of year are wild garlic – fantastic in scrambled egg and omelettes. I also gather very early nettles if there are some, the new spring growth is super-tasty, and put them in soups or have quick-steamed alongside the omelette. Friends also gather chickweed, and burdock but these aren't favourites of mine. I like sheep sorrel and wood sorrel, yarrow, and the wild mustards and winter cress, I'm a confirmed salad-eater so these go very well at a time of year when other salad veg are very scarce. They also work well along with roots in spring pottages and stews.

I enjoy this foraging too because it covers many of the weeds that have sprung up along with spring in my veg and flower beds. They're tougher and stronger than the modern veg my palate prefers and would swamp and strangle them so they need to come out before I sow and transplant my new lettuces and salad greens. Instead of just putting them in the compost it's good to eat some of them too.

Which Plants – Witch Plants

Plants are starting to show their heads above the ground now, the first little spikes of green coming through to show how the Earth is changing.

A student of mine once asked me what herbs and plants she should plant in her garden this year. I'm never very good at doling out orders of what is right, as my dad always answered me in every situation when I asked him for what to do, "That depends ..." and I've got that habit now too! So, the student and me sat together asking her garden what it wanted and needed, and what she would like, then added in my experience. So many wonderful plants came up as we made the list, in fact so many that they split up into different lists. We chuckled at this and she suggested I might well need to make a few different lists based on our experiences of what we – and our gardens – like to grow. We added in what they mean to us and why.

I really don't find dogma useful in this work, nor in my own pagan lifestyle, I always remember what Dad said, that every situation and time, every bit of space-time, is different and needs to be considered and spoken with individually on its own terms. And I'm different every moment too, I'm not quite the same Elen I was a moment ago, nor yesterday, nor last year, so the mental and emotional clothes I wear won't fit now, won't be suitable for me as I am now. And neither will the plants in my garden, nor the garden herself, be the same from one day to the next. So, there's never any right or wrong, only what is appropriate for Now.

Herbs that are good for connecting with the Faer Folk

Lavender – Soothing and healing used for purification and love as opposed to the sex magic of mandrake. I adore lavender and have lots in my garden. It's good for making lavender lemonade, a great summer tipple, and I cut the flowers and add them to my clothes drawers and wardrobes too.

Mugwort – an exceptional herb for helping you do dreamwork and remember your dreams. It helps with divination work as well, usually through giving you true dreams. I always have this in the garden.

Wormwood – a very good herb to help you learn to work with your psychic powers and learn spirit work. Another favourite of mine. Its Latin name is Artemisia absinthium, it's the plant they use to make the drink Absinthe that you may know better as the less potent versions called Ricard and Pernod. It's the plant of Artemis, the magical huntress and guardian of deer, one of my favourite goddesses. Mugwort is another in the artemisia family.

Basil – Protection and Wealth. We all know basil from cooking with tomatoes! But it's also a magical herb, indeed many of our culinary herbs have magical uses too. As well as being good for protection and attracting wealth it makes a great addition to the scents of a herb bundle or what's otherwise known as a smudge stick for burning.

Sage – The Wise One, it gives wisdom. It helps with protection, mostly by helping you understand just what you need protecting from and why you need protection right now at all, very useful things to know as it may just mean a lifestyle change for you rather than something scary like an exorcism! In a similar way it's good for purifying you and your surroundings. I make my own smudge sticks using our native sage herb, not buying in from the other side of the world, our land – like all lands – prefers you to use the plants she grows naturally rather than importing stuff that's not made from her atoms and has a foreign feel. Foreign stuff tends to make your land feel scratchy and irritable so you're likely to have trouble if you give her too much imported stuff.

Lemon Balm – in herbal medicine it's very good for helping the stomach and gut when it gets out of order … in magic work it's very good for helping you heal from stuff you just *can't stomach*! I use it when I've had to be in situations that really annoy me, where everything and everyone are just not my sort of folks, it helps me make a permeable protection film that allows stuff that works well with me through but stops the stuff I don't like.

Rose – Oh! One of my all-time favourite plants. My garden is always full of scented roses. I use the petals in pot pourri, in salads, in sweet dishes, and the rose hips for syrup and cordial. Rose hips contain more vitamin C than an orange. I also use the rose petals for sacred water and tisanes and teas, they work very well when I or my client need to reclaim our sense of beauty and so bring ourselves out of depression. They can also induce tears through the poignancy of their scent, these are healing tears that enable grief and loss to flow away with them.

Valerian – Another dreamer and sleep-aid, much stronger than Mugwort so use it carefully but with similar effects. You may find, if you begin with Mugwort and get used to what happens, that using Valerian sometimes brings a greater clarity and understanding to your dreamwork.

Motherwort – as its name suggests it helps with women's mysteries, childbirth and even the rearing of children, as well as menstruation.

Primrose – Beloved of the Faer Folk. Working with primrose in spring, when they first come into flower, can help you ask the Faer Folk to come to aid and guide you. This is very good to do around Spring when the sun's arc changes and so everything else changes too, as it helps you work-with those changes. It's use in protection is more about helping you let go of fear and so get out of your own way, stop barricading yourself in against shadowy fears, and open up to what the world has to offer you.

Dandelion – The Tooth of the Lion. Its name tells us a lot, there are many times we need the tooth of the lion to help us work our way successfully through all sorts of situations. It's also a good plant to help with digestion, and with fluid retention.

Cat mint – As I'm never without cats my garden is never without catmint, but I love it anyway. It's a beautiful bush plant, covered with scented blue flowers all summer long and adored by bees. It's yet another sleep-aid and dreamer, you can make tisanes and tinctures from it and they're a great help for relaxation and relieving stress.

Spearmint – another digestive plant, stronger and a bit fiercer that Lemon Balm but can do the same jobs. I love the scent of it and it makes great tisanes that ease the whole body usually by getting the digestion working properly. It does similar stuff with the digestion of emotions and thinking too.

Yarrow – one of its country names is Venus Eyebrow because its feathery leaves look a bit like eyebrows. As children we used to stick them over our own eyebrows and say we'd shifted to become fairy folk. It's another plant that attracts the Faer Folk to your garden, they see it and feel into you, see you're likely to be friendly towards them so they come. If you ask them then they will help you in anything you're doing. It's good for putting on wounds too to stop the bleeding.

Flowers

No garden, especially a pagan garden, should be without snowdrops. And another of my favourites is the golden Winter aconites with their yellow buttercup-like flowers, surrounded by leafy bracts from midwinter. The clumps spread quickly to make a dramatic yellow carpet just as the first snowdrops begin to bloom and continues through March. It's perfect for planting beneath trees or naturalising in grass along with the snowdrops and those cyclamen.

Garden Jobs

As I said when I talked about the element for this season, Imbolc is the between place of earth/stone and water, a slithery-place where the soil softens and the water changes from being nearer its solid state of ice and grows into its fluid state of water.

The plants and the garden know this too. As well as the light changes that they calculate and count every day they feel the changes in the soil. We sense this with them and use it as a guide to know what the garden soil needs of us at this time.

It's not always quite the same each year, it always depends

on how the weather has been over the previous season. We sit-with this as part of our celebrations at the beginning/end of each season, asking how things have been for the garden over the last season and what it needs of us as a consequence of that.

But one thing is sure ... as the plants move from concentrating on the parts of themselves below ground to those above the ground the need us to pay attention to the soil.

Early Spring Planning

As Patti Wittington said in her blog,

> "In the early spring, many of us who follow earth-based spiritual paths begin planning our gardens for the coming season. The very act of planting, of beginning new life from seed, is a ritual and a magical act in itself. To cultivate something in the black soil, see it sprout and then bloom, is to watch a magical working unfold before our very eyes. The plant cycle is intrinsically tied to so many earth-based belief systems that it should come as no surprise that the magic of the garden is one well worth looking into."

In the early spring, many of us who follow earth-based spiritual paths begin planning our gardens for the coming season. The very act of planting, of beginning new life from seed, is a ritual and a magical act in itself. To cultivate something in the black soil, see it sprout and then bloom, is to watch a magical working unfold before our very eyes. The plant cycle is intrinsically tied to so many earth-based belief systems that it should come as no surprise that the magic of the garden is one well worth looking into. Let's look at some of the folklore and traditions that surround gardening and planting magic.

Pay Attention to Your Soil

Soil again ... it's not possible to overemphasize the importance of good soil.

Your garden will grow best in nutrient-rich, well-drained, weeded, and loosened (non-compacted) soil.

At Midwinter you gave the garden as much organic matter as you had from your compost bins. Hopefully, you were also able to get some farmyard manure from somewhere, there are several places you can get it online and more garden centres are selling it nowadays too. Cow manure is the best but chicken manure is good too as long as it's well composted; you shouldn't use it fresh as it really does burn then, scorching plants and the soil ... and so harming, maybe killing, all the good wildlife in the soil that helps the plants to grow.

If you have a cat, dog, rabbits, hamsters, birds, any animals that live with you, put their dung in your compost bins too when you clean out litters and such. It all helps the compost and adds goodness to it – much better than dumping it on the council for them to dispose of.

Now, at Imbolc, is the time to check how the compost and manure you put on at Midwinter has gone into the ground. The worms and soil wildlife have been working on it for the past season and you'll see a difference already.

Soils are... Young to Very, Very Old

It's really hard to say just when some soils were born. Some are young, but many are very, very old. The current best guess from geologists is that the oldest soils may be in Australia; the land-forms there have been stable for a very long time so some of the soils there have aged undisturbed for several million years. New soils, on the other hand, are born with every landslide, volcanic eruption, or glacial retreat. Mother Earth is continually recycling her skin.

Soils also change over time, they're all affected by a host of biological, chemical, and physical processes; and our gardening and farming are actually a huge part of that. In 2010, the World

Bank reported that a massive 37.7 percent of the world's total land area was agricultural land. That's over 1/3rd of the Earth's surface that we change and mess with through agriculture and farming alone, never mind our building and mining efforts. We humans radically change the Earth by what we do and not often for her betterment. As gardeners we can do our tiny bit to change that and, as pagans, we know she does appreciate it and it is worthwhile.

There are all sorts of soils; their variety and the number of soil formation processes that work on different sorts of rock, under different climates, the different shapes and features of land surfaces, and the biological conditions over time give rise to the vast diversity of soils on Earth. Soil formation creates a dizzying array of soil horizons. Some soils harden irreversibly upon being repeatedly wetted and dried. Some contain pyrite which, when exposed to oxygen, can produce so much sulfuric acid that it kills plants and fish; something our mining contributes to though most of us don't know. Some soils have so much calcium carbonate in them it literally forms a rock-like layer in the middle of a soil. Soil scientists are always looking into all this so they can tell us just what our activities are doing.

The U.S. system, called Soil Taxonomy (soils.usda.gov/technical/classification/taxonomy/), groups soils into 12 broad orders at the most general level, and more than 19,000 soil series at the most detailed level (Ahrens & Arnold 1999). The International Union of Soil Sciences has developed a system called the World Reference Base, which has 32 Reference Soil Groups (http://www.fao.org/nr/land/soils/soil/en/).

Soils are Biological Bliss & Perfect Ecosystems

If you like life, you'll love soils. Millions and millions of small, medium, and large organisms live in soils and those include mammals, birds, insects, and protozoa. But the greatest biodiversity lies in the soil microbes, billions, trillions, of bacteria, fungi, and microscopic beasties live in the soil. A teaspoon of good, rich soil can contain one billion bacteria. We know very little as yet about the diversity of soil microbes, and that's partly because they *are* so diverse, but soil microbiologists are working hard to understand them and their diversity and function.

Soils are one of the greatest ecosystem service providers on Earth. They store and provide water for plants; prevent floods by transferring water slowly to streams and groundwater; filter, provide remedies for environmental damage and pollutants. They cycle and recycle nutrients and waste matter, transforming the waste into stuff that makes new plants and animals (and us!); it also stores those transformed atoms away for later use, and so prevents their leaching away to ground and surface waters. Soils provide habitat for a vast diversity of life; they take up and release important gases, including oxygen and greenhouse gases. Unfortunately, human activity means many of these ecosystem services are being lost as we degrade the soils and they are lost through erosion due to our bright ideas of progress/ improvement. As pagan gardeners we can do our little bit to help stop and reverse that.

Celebration

Imbolc – we pronounce it as *imolck*, with the "b" silent – is the time when winter gives way to spring. As gardeners, we see, hear and smell the difference when *spring has sprung*, the birdsong changes, the air smells different, even the soil itself has a different scent as it warms up. The first bulbs, especially the snowdrops, push their way up through the often-frozen soil.

We celebrate Imbolc on 31st January and 1st Feb; we tell stories about the meeting of Ceridwen, as Lady of Winter who we met at Midwinter, passing her Cup of Life to Bridey (Bridget), as Lady of Spring, to carry forward into the season of Imbolc. The snowdrop is her flower and we always have some for this feast as it comes into our stories. Our stories celebrate the awakening of the

Goddess after she's given birth to the Sun at midwinter; we watch the first stirrings of life after the winter and feel into the energy of the land. For our ancestors, the significance of Imbolc would have been the beginning of the ground thaw. It is the time to prepare for the planting season — to survey the land, take an inventory of tools, and make any repairs or modifications that will be needed.

The snowdrop is significant for gardeners too as it helps us gauge what the land knows the weather is going to do for the next six weeks. We watch the date when snowdrop flowers first appear in our gardens, maybe discuss with friends and neighbours how theirs are doing and compare how high up we each are, which direction most winds come from and if we're sheltered, how much sunlight our patch gets and what sort of soil we each have. It's a time for thinking about how we're going to grow things in the coming year and, like the old gardeners and farmers, a time for checking over our gardening tools, making sure they're clean and sharp, mending those we can and getting new for those we can't.

It's also a time for checking fences and hedges, and planting the last of any new trees or hedging plants the land needs. This time of first new growth is the last chance we have for helping newly planted trees and bushes to root well before they need to deal with the sun of summer. At Imbolc, there's usually enough rain – sometimes too much! – to keep the young plants happy, while the lengthening days and concurrent increase in the amount of sunlight, helps to warm the soil from out of its winter sleep and so feed the newly planted roots.

Meditation – Earth Breathing

There are 3 *breathing* cycles the Earth does throughout the year, two come under the aegis of the sun and one the moon. We'll look at Moon-Cycling in a later chapter but here's a bit about the sun's cycles and a little exercise you could do to help yourself reconnect with the cycles of the Earth and Sun.

The annual sun-cycle, is the Earth's orbit around the sun that takes a whole year. It splits into halves and quarters, the halves are the two solstices, Midwinter and Midsummer at each of which the sun's arc changes from getting higher from Midwinter to getting lower from Midsummer. Each half is also split into two by the equinoxes, Spring and Autumn when, for one day only we have equal amounts of light and dark.

While we have more darkness than light each day – from Autumn to Spring - the Earth breathes IN. When we have more light than dark each day – from Spring to Autumn – the Earth breathes OUT. She does a similar thing each day too only in the daily case she … Breathes IN from midday to midnight, and Breathes OUT from midnight to midday. To get the feel of this here's a good little breathing exercise you could do each day to help you reconnect.

Stand in your garden, be relaxed, and feel your breathing, feel your breath flowing in and out.
As you breathe IN, feel a thread growing down out of you. Feel yourself travel down the thread, going deep through the soil and rocks, deep into the heart of the Earth.
As you breathe OUT, feel yourself travel back up that thread, up your spine and see a new thread grow out of the top of your head. feel the thread go up through the atmosphere, out across space, and deep into the heart of the Sun.
As you breathe IN again, feel yourself travel down that thread, across space, down through the atmosphere, down your spine, down through the rocks to the heart of the Earth again.
As you breathe OUT, feel yourself travel UP the thread again, through the earth, up your spine, and out across space to the heart of the Sun.
Repeat this as often as you like,
breathing IN as you travel between Sun and Earth,
breathing OUT as you travel between Earth and Sun.

if you do this several times a week, just for a moment or two, you'll feel a real difference to your connection with the natural world, and the Earth and the Sun.

Spring Equinox

Season

Spring Equinox is the first moment of balance in the year, the first time there's equal light and dark just for one day. I feel that as being very special. In the old ways as I was brought up it was a divination time. I remember getting up in the dark on the morning of Spring and going next door with my step-mum, Vera, to the older woman, Mrs Webber, who lived there. The three of us went to the cottage where my Aunt Ida lived, then along to the square where we met up with several other village women. Then we all went up the hill behind the village. There was a little trickling spring near the top, it would dry up most summers but at the end of January it was full of water, and either Mrs Webber or Aunt Ida would fill a small silver bowl from the spring. As a child I always felt the bowl was magic, it lived in a box at the back of the Welsh Dresser in our kitchen and only came out for special occasions and Imbolc was one of those. We all sat round in a circle in the pre-dawn light, well wrapped up as it was usually perishing cold at that time back in the 1950s. The women began to hum, I and another girl, daughter of one of the old ones, joined in, the humming was quite trance like. Slowly the sun rose out of the woods below us and its first rays caught the water in the silver bowl. Mrs Webber, Aunt Ida and old Granny Clitheroe from the village bakery could see things in the bright water then, and I found I could too. I saw pictures, later as we went through the year I found the pictures came true.

The sun's rays would quickly move on, the bright water effect only lasted a few moments, then it was over and the thermoses of tea came out so everyone could have a warming up and a couple of biscuits. As we sipped our tea, Vera would note down what each of us had seen in the Shadow Book, then we'd all keep an eye out for the thing to happen over the coming year. There would be things about the gardens, the vegetables and fruit and the crops on the farms, several of the women were farmer's wives and mothers and we all gardened so it was good to know what might well happen over the year so we could be ready. Sometimes some of the things would be unfortunate or sad things, I saw Granny Clitheroe's death one year and so did she at the same time, she talked about it with me later and it really helped me not to be afraid of dying.

I know people in many parts of Britain who still do this ceremony now and I still have that silver bowl ...

Element

Water is the element that works with Spring. The leaves are coming on well in the plants now and they're full of water. Water is vital for the plants as its one of the three things they use to feed themselves and to give us oxygen – water, sunlight and carbon dioxide (CO_2). The plant draws the water up from the ground, the sunlight is (hopefully) up there in the sky, and the CO_2 is in the air all around. It's worth remembering we wouldn't live without plants to make the oxygen for us.

We wouldn't live long without water either. I think the longest anyone has survived without water is three or four days. It's the life-blood of the Earth, all her creatures and plants need it.

Altar

While I still do the silver bowl meditation most years that's not the garden altar I use for Spring. I have a pond in the garden and it's one of the focal points for my Spring altar but not the main one. At spring I always find myself turning east to the point on the hills where the sun rises at the spring equinox.

My kitchen faces east so I see this every morning as I make the first pot of tea for the day. Outside the kitchen is the yard – that's not the garden here in Britain but a work area with hard standing where we have the rotary washing line, the woodshed, my gardening shed, Paul's Man Shed, things like that. I have the wormery out there too and the hot-bin for composting really tough pernicious stuff like the excess nettles and hog weed! I also have the bokashi bins out there too. My potting and plant tables are out in the yard too, where I pot up and grow on wee plants until they're strong enough to go out in the garden, so it's very much a spring-place, about springtime work and things.

The eastern wall of the yard is about a metre high and the wall is made of dressed local stone from the quarry pit in the hill to the north behind the house. In the wall there's a seat-like slab of stone, really attractive so I use this as my Spring altar. East and Spring equinox relate in our old ways as it's the first day of the year when the sun rises due east.

The altar always has a bowl of water on it along with a pot of garden soil, I think all my altars have this to remind me to relate as strongly as I can with the spirit of place where I live. At this season the water focuses me on the element of water that brings the soil awake again after the cold, dark inner workings of winter. I add some herbs to the bowl of water, looking for whatever is first up in the garden, often it's some sage and mint in my climate. I add flower petals too, like calendula (the old pot-marigold) and a daffodil trumpet, again whatever has shown itself at the time. And I put a tea-light in an old earthenware plant pot then jam the pot solid with some large pebbles – we get a lot of wind up where I am and I don't want the whole shebang blowing all over the garden.

I light the tea-light the day before equinox, again on the day and again on the day after, greeting the springtime and the garden spirit, and asking that they show me what they most need me to do in the garden right now.

I find doing a little ritual, finding the herbs and flowers, taking a spoonful of soil and a cup of water, and lighting the candle really helps me focus on the change of season, acknowledging it and recognising it. Paying attention ...

Asking, answers and paying attention

It can sound quite nuts to do all this asking and greeting and listening for answers to those who've never done it … but it isn't. people say, "Oh! I can't do that. Nothing ever speaks to me." I've been teaching people, enabling and helping them to do just this since the 1970s, that's the best part of 50 years now, and just about every time I work with someone, they quite quickly find they can and do ask otherworld and hear the answers. The usual difficulty is that they been inured and inculcated with the concept that to do this means they're not normal, mad in some way, mentally deranged. Of course, nobody wants that! Once they discover they can do it they get a wonderful smile on their faces, are thrilled. And so am I, it's so good to watch someone shed all the old rubbish they were taught and that trapped them all their lives up to then. They're so happy to be free at last, and that makes my heart sing.

You can do this too. Really, I mean it. Everyone has this ability, it's just that we've been convinced by those we call authority figures that we don't. None of us has to live by other people's scripts, we can all let go of them when we wish to but it helps to have some encouragement from someone you trust.

Our hunter-gatherer ancestors from fifty or a hundred thousand years ago could, they needed to in order to live and they lived very well, a few hours hunting and foraging each week and the rest of the time to produce beautiful things like the incredible cave art, or the swimming reindeer (go to the British Museum site for pictures) that were carved from a mammoth's tusk 14,000 years ago. They had time to watch the heavens and learn the stars, learn about trees and animals, the tides of the sea, the fish and the birds. How much time to do these things does modern life allow most people? Not a lot usually …

Each and every one of us can reclaim those old skills if we want to. They lie hidden and inert within us until we decide it's time to waken them … and then? We find our lives are enormously expanded and far more fun. And that goes for gardening too.

Plants

Herbs

Spring Equinox is the promise of Imbolc finally arrived! The wheel of the year has turned and although wind, rain, and the last chill breath of winter may still hold some sway the plants and trees are budding up and the birds are singing their hearts out. And there are many herbal allies we can work with in springtime.

Dandelion – is one I especially love. Its name means the tooth of the lion and for me it's *the* Sun Flower, far more so than the big sunflowers many people grow later in the year. It comes up now at spring and provides masses of much needed pollen for the newly awake insects to feed themselves up on so they get strong to come and pollinate all our fruit and veg plants. Bees and other pollinators really need this early boost and dandelions give and give and give, they're so wonderfully generous with their flowers.

Seeing them, gold against the new spring green, lifts my heart too, makes me feel more awake and alive. I use all parts of the plant – roots, leaves and flowers. It's got lots of country names like Bitterwort, fairy clock and fortune teller for the spherical seedheads – who hasn't blown them away and wished, especially as children? I've heard it called swine's snout though I've never known why, and milk witch or wort for its milky, juicy sap.

It's a great detoxifier and gently cleanses of the body and digestive tract, it can also help with fluid retention. I make dandelion flower tisane for that stagnant feeling I get at the end of winter, it's like a bodily spring-clean. Lion's tooth, Dandelion, a bold, toothy ally that grows just about everywhere and offers itself to help is a spring-clean for the new season.

Dandelion helps with the transition of the spring equinox

that can feel a bit like a see-saw as the balance shifts from more darkness to more light. Our bodies instinctively know it's happening even if our modern minds rubbish the idea and dandelion helps us walk through this time and so get our body, mind and feelings more in balance.

As well as tisanes, I add the fresh young leaves to salads, and juice them up in the juicer with other herbs and veggies too. The leaves are great in stir-fries as well, and in soups. If you also roast the root in the oven then grind it up in the coffee grinder you may enjoy it as a form of coffee. I also make dandelion vinegar by mixing the root, fresh or dried, in raw apple cider vinegar and letting it steep for a month. Taste to check it's ready then strain it off and use it with salads. Folklore tells us that to drink a tea of dandelion root will awaken the third eye, and if you carry a dandelion flower on your person your wishes may well be granted.

Burdock root – although not a favourite of mine, is another herb for the spring … if you can make the effort to dig it up, I freely admit I'm very bad at this! it is a good cleansing herb though and I suspect I should make the effort more often. The root is bitter, sweet, and oily. It's very good for imbalances with the liver and gallbladder when you get both indigestion and constipation, as can happen at the end of winter. It's also good for dry, flaky skin, acne and rashes and can help with blood sugar imbalances too.

Nettles – are another of my favourites. They're extremely good medicine and young spring nettles are very good for waking up our bodies from their winter break. They jog the muscles, fill us up with lots of vitamins and minerals, and ease aching joints. Again, I use them as a tisane, sometimes as a hair-rinse, and I make nettle soup, use them instead of spinach and quick-fry them in butter to go with other dishes. My colleague Fiona Dove and I had an especially good meal of foraged limpets from a beach on north Orkney and young nettle tops all fried in butter and Orkney ale. Yummmm! And so deliciously fresh as we'd gathered them all ourselves an hour before.

Nettles help the liver build blood proteins and support a healthy immune system, as well as being good for hair loss, brittle nails, dull skin, anaemia, and general feelings of stagnation.

Veg: Grow What You Love: Negotiation

What's the point of growing vegetables you don't like to eat? Let your palate dictate your choices when choosing your crops, but try to stay open to planting at least a couple new vegetables each year to keep your home garden a bit more exciting. The last thing you want is to have your garden feel like a chore rather than a source of inspiration and relaxation.

So, although you had a good sit-with and ponder at Midwinter and have likely been mulling it over in all the weeks since then, now is a good time to really finalise what veg you want to grow this coming year.

I always base this around what my tummy wants. Unfortunately, I suffer from several autoimmune diseases, rheumatoid arthritis (RA), Sjogren's syndrome and latent IBS and diabetes type 2. Bad eating, for me that meant eating any form of grains, breads, pasta, couscous, etc and dried pulses, gave me what's known as "leaky gut" and that wrecked my immune system and set off all these conditions. Good eating – staying completely away from any sort of grain and pseudo grain and all pulses – has enabled me to get rid of the IBS and the diabetes, and massively reduce the effects of both Sjogren's and RA. In consequence I now follow a paleo-keto diet and am pretty fit but this means I hardly eat any roots; I grow some green beans because in moderation I'm OK with them every now and again but otherwise no pulses. Green leaves and fruit, plus good organic meat and fish, are the order of the day so this is what I grow in the garden.

It's actually amazing all the salad-stuff you can grow all year round with the aid of a small unheated polytunnel ... and lots of mulch and compost. So, because of my preferences this is what I grow. Spend time yourself really getting down to the nitty gritty of the veg and fruit you really enjoy and grow those. Don't grow stuff just because a TV programme or a book tells you it's a good idea. Like I said before there's absolutely no point in growing what you don't enjoy.

Flowers

Spring brings on the first flush of blooms to thrill the heart. Ones I love at springtime are ...

Crocus – one of the first flowers to poke their heads up in the spring. I love seeing great drifts of them across green grass or under the edges of trees, I've not yet achieved drift in the garden here at Bryngwyn but then I've only been here a year, Give it another year or three and then ...

The only crocus that gives us the herb saffron is Crocus sativus. It comes from its wild ancestor, Crocus cartwrightianus, which is now extremely rare due to a combination of habitat loss and over-collection to make money from selling the strands. You can grow this yourself but if you do, you'll quickly realise just how many you need to grow to fill one of the herb jars you bought (and thought so expensive) in the supermarket! The saffron crocus blooms in the autumn and so is not a contender for spring beauty. It is beautiful though with purple petals, yellow stamens and a three-part red-orange stigma that is what becomes the saffron strands.

Daffodil – I can't imagine spring without daffodils. They come in all shades and colour and sizes but the ones I love most of all are the tiny Hooped Petticoat variety, they're native to southern and western France, Portugal, and Spain, not Britain but I still adore them.

The only species of narcissus (daffodil) native to Britain is the tiny Lent Lily, *Narcissus pseudonarcissus*. They thrive in damp woodland and pasture and are vigorous growers, well able to naturalise in dappled shade and open woodland. I've begun a patch in my woodland corner here that I call the Wolery after Owl's House in Winnie the Pooh.

Forsythia – Another of my loves is forsythia. I have a small hedge of it by the front gate and it's such a pleasure to watch as the brilliant gold flowers catch the spring sunshine. You need to clip it back every year after flowering as it easily grows tall so the lovely blossoms tower over your head where you can neither smell nor see them. I feel a bit guilty about having it though as it's an exotic from North America, and of very little use to wildlife; it has no berries for the birds and is not a host plant for either butterflies or moths. But it does gladden my heart and there's only a wee bit of it. And its multiplicity of thin stems makes it a good wind filter as well as good shelter for birds and insects from the severe winds that blow around here.

Hyacinth – these were named for Hyakinthos, a Greek hero who was beloved by Apollo, he was killed by accident by his lover, Apollo, while he was teaching Hyakinthos to throw the discus. It has a wonderful scent and I usually have some right by the kitchen door so I smell them whenever I go outside during their season. Another non-native that I love.

Violet – I love violets, another native plant that's also beloved of bees and other insects. Sweet violets are widespread across the UK, commonly found in woods and hedgerows. They're used in herbal medicine to treat headaches, depression and insomnia. They have been used to make perfume throughout history, going right back to Classical Greece, and were also used as early household deodorants since medieval Britain. They're edible, and are often candied and used to decorate cakes. They can also be added to salads or used as a garnish.

It's easy to confuse sweet violets with common dog violet (Viola riviniana) as they're almost identical in appearance, but completely unscented. In flower magic, the dried flowers are used in incense to bring sweet dreams and restful sleep. Some people sew them into a pillow to make Dream Pillows.

Safety Tip
Remember that some plants can be toxic to pets. The RSPCA (or the relevant organisation in your country) will have website that give you the relevant information about toxic and non-toxic plants where you live.

Garden Jobs
Spring equinox heralds the busiest season in the garden particularly for the vegetable and fruit grower, but for those of us who grow flowers it's almost as hectic. There are seeds to be sown, plants to be transplanted or planted out for the first time, quite a lot of pruning to be done and the weeds! The weeds, the plants in the wrong place, will very naturally take off and grow like mad now spring has sprung, so we're always trying to keep on top of that job.

With seed sowing and veggies, you're probably like me and will already have begun that, filling up window ledges with trays full of pots containing the veg seeds you can't yet sow outside because the soil is still too cold.

Here are two things I do to help ease the congestion around the house ...

- Cover the beds to keep the heat and moisture in. I usually use cardboard from old boxes collected through the previous year because a) cardboard breathes and lets the rain through, and b) because it's made from wood-pulp it rots down and gives its energy back to the soil. And c) recycling it means less waste to throw away!

- Have a small polytunnel that grows my winter salad and keeps the new-sown spring seeds warm and protected.

I don't buy potting compost either. Around Imbolc is when the moles come up and start building their worm-larders again – that's what molehills are, the soil turned up as mole creates a new worm-larder. Molehills are another sign of Imbolc for us ... and they're also an excellent source of well-turned local soil just right for seed sowing and potting on. and they're free, all you need do is go out with a bucket and collect the soil.

Some gardening books deplore this and tell you how unhealthy it is. It's actually fine, my gardening Uncle Perce, Aunt Ida's husband, taught me to do this way back in the 1950s. What do these gardening books think we all did before commercial compost was available?

So, the Spring Equinox season is very much about ...

- tending and caring for your soil
- sowing seeds
- keeping on top of the weeds (and don't forget to eat some of them)
- pruning the trees and bushes that need it in spring – any good gardening book will tell you which these are, and you can look it up on Google.
- And if you grow rhubarb, (I do and I love it) you should have begun harvesting it by the equinox, it's a lovely fresh fruit to be able to pick so early in the year.

Another garden job that "springs" to mind – sorry about the pun! – is caring for the birds. I do this all year round but in spring they're mating and beginning to nest. Many species are just then returning from overwintering abroad and need the extra help after their long journey.

Just along from the end of the yard wall we have a big buddleia bush that gets very little pruning as it's one of the main hideouts for the birds on their way to the feeders. The little song birds need refuge points in their flight and the buddleia bush is one of the last of those before they have to expose themselves to predators to get to the food. We can see the bush from the kitchen, bathroom, my bedroom and Paul's study and it makes an excellent place to watch. It's like it flowers and fruits small birds as they all dive into it then out to the feeder, and then back to the buddleia again. We're able to do good birds counts for the BTO (British Trust for Ornithology) by watching that bush.

Every place I've ever lived we've had feeders, water sources and nesting places that are safe and sheltered. I always feed the birds throughout the winter too, in fact throughout the year, on fat, seeds and peanuts. We've messed up their habitats so much in the past fifty years it feels obligatory to me to offer some return and recompense. And every season has its harder moments for the birds – winter with a scarcity of food and the same in spring especially after a long flight back to Britain. Then there's mating, nest-building, laying eggs which needs a lot of food-energy, sitting on the eggs which means you can't go off and feed. Then there's chick rearing which uses a helluva lot of energy so feeding then makes it easier for more young birds to make it to adulthood. And after chick-rearing comes moulting, changing all your feathers which makes you feel itchy and down so an easy source of food really helps. Then comes autumn and harvest when there is hopefully an abundance of wild food, certainly the birds I guardian come far less frequently to the feeders for a couple of months. But I feed them anyway as many birds have a long autumn flight ahead to warmer climes for the winter and need all the energy they can get to prepare for a flight to, say, Africa. And then we're back to winter again. And anyway, it's just so delightful to see them in the yard and in the garden.

Celebration

Equinoxes are times of balance but just what is balance? Most people think of balance as something with the weight evenly distributed on both sides of a fulcrum but this is way off the beam. Dancers, acrobats and athletes know better, balance can just as easily be standing on one leg.

Balance in the garden is worth thinking about. And evenness, regularity, like a pair of candle sticks one either end of the mantelpiece rarely makes you look twice or your heart sing. The joy of beauty usually comes from unevenness, a balance that is like the labile poise of a dancer poised on one toe and about to fall into the next move. It's a tiny still-point, a moment of glorious action frozen for a that instant.

Think about photos that really make you go wow. The footballer at the moment of kicking just as the ball takes off, the tennis player at the full stretch of a service, the child in the middle of a set of cartwheels, a horse leaping a fence at full stretch. They're all amazing, wonderful. They all make you stop and maybe catch your breath for a moment. Your garden can be like that too.

I always make gardens into a set of spaces. It's like when you walk through a wood; one minute you're in a deep shadowy path with trees overhanging, mysterious and suggesting gnomes and fairies, then you round a corner and you're in a little glade with sunshine and a single bright rose bush flowering and giving off her scent. Or you cross a patch of lawn, and there, behind a big bush, is a little jewel of a pond. Or you come round to the other side of the house and there's a bigger pond with a waterfall splashing down into it, even the sound is cooling and calming.

You can use statuary like this too, and things like an old gate set in a path, strange-shaped bits of old timber and tree branches. Use your imagination and also look on Google and in gardening books, visit open gardens. You'll find ideas to set the balance for your garden.

And the first thing to think about is what really makes your heart sing in the garden, what do you really enjoy doing most when you're out there? Maybe it's running water, or masses of colour, shady spots and beautiful trees, growing your own veg and herbs. You might be interested in herbs as medicine too and so want to begin growing your own medicine-garden. Do you really enjoy just sitting, listening to the birds and the wind, watching the grasses blowing gently, smelling wonderful scents, watching the butterflies, dragonflies and bees? All things to consider.

And what about your garden? What would it like to be? What would it like to do? What would it like you to do when you're in it? What does it need? It's worth sitting there in a favourite quiet spot and asking the spirit of place of your garden all those questions. Have a book and pen with you so you can jot down notes of what the garden spirit puts into your mind.

To work well, you and your garden need to be in balance … but remember balance that gives you joy is about the moment poised between two other moments. Balance has flow, movement, and is what we call *labile* in dance – I used to be a dancer. The way you and your garden work together will be much better if you allow for this flow and movement between your needs and the garden's.

I've built lots of gardens in my life, one even growing out of a piece of field, what you'd think of as a blank canvas but actually it wasn't. The field was used to being a field, it had lots of field plants, and field-style soil, but when I sat with its spirit and offered it the choice of changes as I thought of and dreamed of how things could be the spirit leapt at the offer. Between us we made a lovely place that kept habitat for the critters that had always lived there but added to it too, so it got deeper and more profound in some ways. The critters loved it too, we got even more wildlife when the garden was made than had been there before I began. And all by sitting-with the spirit of place, asking, talking, suggesting …

Beltane

Season

Beltane is the ancient name for the May Day fire festival, the name comes from the god Bel – meaning the bright one – and is one of the two poles of the magical year, when the gates to the land of the Faer are most open to travellers.

Beltane celebrates the Celtic sun-god and Allfather, his name means Bright Fire. Our ancestors well understood how vital the sun is for all life. Without the sun there would be no life so we thank and honour the sun, thanking him for nurturing the summer growing season for beasts and plants.

Our ancestors' wisdom only gets proven more and more as we come to understand better and better, through science, just how important our own personal star, the sun, is for us. As indeed are all stars. Way back in the 1960s Joni Mitchell sang, "We are stardust ...", and she was so, so right! What we are made of comes from the death of stars, neutron stars, we are indeed stardust!

Our British seasons come in two flavours, those of the goddess and those of the god, always the Lady and the Lord dance together through the year and through the seasons. The four goddess seasons are about the Earth - Samhain, Imbolc, Beltane and Lammas. The four god-seasons are about the Sun - Midwinter, Spring, Midsummer and Autumn. The Sun-god seasons fall on the 2 solstices and the 2 equinoxes while the Earth-goddess seasons fall between them.

Element

Like Imbolc, Beltane is a threshold place between the elements, this time between water and fire. In our old ways the coming together of water and fire is an especially magical thing. In the everyday world we use water to quench fire, and fire to transform water from a fluid into a gas (steam), they're at opposite poles, the one kills the other – or does it always? When they can come together, they create pure ... and very explosive ... magic.

Did you know, for instance, that ice can make a lens to create fire, if it's clear? And don't ever throw water on a chip pan that's on fire! There're loads of amazing videos of people demonstrating what happens with that one ... talk about explosions!

On a more serious note, what's rocket fuel made from? Hydrogen and oxygen... combine them you create an explosion.... and water. That's incredible magic to me, and it's about enabling us to explore the universe, not just by going to the moon but incredible things like the Hubble Space Telescope that's enabled us to learn so much. And now Hubble's "son", the new James Webb Space Telescope that is able to show even more of the universe than Hubble – and I was continually stunned by Hubble's images as well as what the scientists were able to discover from them. It's expected to have as profound and far-reaching an impact on astrophysics as did Hubble.

So, Beltane really does hold both the energies of fire and water as we tell in our mythos. And this not only opens the gates between the worlds of the Faer Folk and our everyday world but now between our Earth and the rest of the Universe! For me, knowing more about the workings of the universe helps me with my gardening because particle physics as well as our old ways shows us that we truly are all intimately connected with everything else.

Altar

My Beltane altar is actually a Moon Gate in the south-east corner of the garden, a blacksmith friend over in Wales made it for me years ago and it came with me (much to the confusion of the removal-men!) when we moved up to Shropshire. It's very simple, a circle of steel held between two simple uprights, and I've asked honeysuckle, passion flower and climbing nasturtiums to twine round it. Indeed, when we first came to view this house there was the honeysuckle growing up beside this big old hardy fuchsia at the corner-entrance to the garden. The honeysuckle shouted to me, "Hey! I want that Moon Gate of yours!" Well that sorted that then didn't it?

So, the Moon Gate is my altar. It already has plants twining it and a stone slab as its Stepping Stone that leads you through, I set the tea-light in the earthenware flower-pot on that step for the night before, the day of, and the day after Beltane as a focus for me to remember the season. With the flower-pot-candle I set a bowl of water so I have fire and water on my altar. But I don't attempt to make rocket fuel!

Incidentally, we all get things like the honeysuckle shouting to me … it's just a case of us learning not to dismiss it as we've likely been taught to. Communicating with the other realms of nature really is a natural trait for humans, it's just that our modern culture has squashed it to such a degree many people are really scared to believe they have. OK guys, time to climb out of that box and smell the coffee!

Plants

Herbs

Wyrts, Worts & Weeds, it feels like this is good moment to talk about them in this season. The word "wort" come from the Old English word *wyrt* and means a plant, herb or root. The word *weed* is also from an Old English word, *wod*, and that means herb!

My gardening Uncle Perce always told me that a weed is just a plant in the wrong place from a human point of view … not necessarily the perspective of the plant, nor the spirit of place! As he also taught me to talk with plants and learn directly from them I've always found his advice very good, it really does work if you're willing to spend the time discovering, direct from the nettle, just why it's decided to invade your cabbage patch. There will be a reason. Did you know that the soil, after nettles have been growing in it, is some of the best soil on Earth? It is, really. The nettle roots do amazing things to open up clagged particles of soil. They help break up compacted clay – especially if you've been rotavating the veg garden every spring and so pound the soil below the rotavator blades into the sort of surface we had for the big pool in the last garden! It's an old practice you can do to make a pond without using a liner and very handy if you've been able to make your pond over a natural spring as we were. You "puddle" the clay, it's excellent fun for kids as it means you get in there, in the hole, with the wet clay and puddle it with your feet, and kids will love doing it with bare feet. As clay's slippery when wet there's lot of fun falling over and getting seriously dirty, a great way to spend a summer afternoon and then finish up with a good barbecue, and a shower!

But … is this really what you want for your veg garden? The puddled clay makes such a good, seamless liner that no water gets through from either direction, either from below or above, except for where you've piped the spring in. Your veggies won't like that. They need to draw up water from deep in the ground, and that's part of what those magic fungi, the mycorrhiza, do. If you pound the soil, compact it, so no water can get to the plants, you screwed up quite well. So, the nettles may come in to help the plants and the soil get back into their proper balance. Their tiny, thread-like roots wriggle their way onto the compacted mess and free it up, so the water can get through again. We had to persuade the nettles in the last garden not to mess up the pond this way and so kill all the pond plants and wee water beasties who lived there. They'd got the hang of it by the end of the second year – completely without chemicals – and so all got back into the new balance of having the pond the spirit of place had asked for as soon as we got there. It just takes a bit of time and patience and effort.

So, the worts and wyrts and weeds all have a purpose. As a follower of the old ways I do my best to learn that purpose, and not fall into the common habit of thinking that if I didn't buy it at the garden centre it's a nasty weed and has to go.

The naming of plants can be a difficult matter – to misquote TS Eliot's poem the Naming of Cats. Humans have been doing it since we could speak and likely before when we were chattering moneys, we've never lost the chatter-habit it's so deep in our natures. Unlike most other critters who use telepathic-like means, and that includes trees and plants as well as the "mobile" critters like animals, birds and insects, we humans use vocal sounds that we form into words. So, we need "names" in order to tell each other things, and to name the plants we like and grow in our gardens.

The words *Weed* and *Wort/Wyrt* contain value-judgments about the plants, often along the lines of is this a useful plant, one I like, one I dislike and seems useless to me, or even a dangerous plant. And our modern value-judgements are often not the same as those our ancestors made.

Wort is a non-woody plant that has medicinal value. Our ancestors sometimes worked with the idea that if a plant looked like some part of the human body then it would be good for that body part. Think of lungwort, spleenwort, liverwort and ribwort. Ribwort is the slender-leaved variety of plantain, Plantago lanceolata, and it really does work on the ribs as I can attest. Earlier this year I fell and cracked a rib bone, intensely painful and made moving and even breathing very difficult. Fortunately, I have herb-wife friends who pointed me at making a "plaster" – a mushy mess – if plantain leaves and getting my husband to stick the concoction on my cracked rib. Within 3 days the rib was so much better I could breathe and even laugh again. I had to be careful for a few weeks, and kept applying a new plaster every day for another week but now it's better, healed far more quickly than a friend down the lane who cracked her rib in a similar way last year. So, don't knock worts and wyrts, they do work despite what the Pharm companies tell us! There's lots and lots of worts, herbs. Here's a few names for you …

Feverfew, feverwort (triosteum, also called horse gentian or wild coffee) and tetterwort (chelidonium majus, aka the greater celandine). Then there's bellwort, birthwort, bladderwort, bloodwort (aka bloodroot), butterwort, figwort, glasswort, liverwort, lousewort, lungwort, milkwort, moneywort, mugwort, nipplewort, pennywort, pepperwort, pilewort, pipewort, quillwort, rupturewort, sandwort, spiderwort, spleenwort, St. John's wort, and stonewort.

Likely names like spiderwort and lousewort mean these plants are helpful to work with any excess and imbalance between us and these creatures. Others like bellwort, figwort and moneywort maybe get their names from the shape of their leaves or flowers. I'm not a herb-wife so I don't know these things.

Weeds are unfortunate plants that humans came to consider useless, or maybe prone to aggressive growth that chokes out modern crops and herbs humans think are useful. Some writers say their country names like bindweed, carpetweed, fireweed, hawkweed, horseweed, Joe-pye-weed, knotweed, milkweed, ragwort, pigweed, smartweed and sneezewort, show how we think them useless and aggressive but I'm really unconvinced of this. Sneezewort does work with sneezing, sometimes to help you clear your throat and lungs. Bindweed is really useful to bind things up with, I'm a wild-camper and go off hiking in wilderness places and many are the occasions bindweed has helped instead of modern paracord or string. I think we've forgotten again what our ancestors knew of these plants; it will be good if we relearn that old knowing, and then the names will make more sense too.

Biologists and ecologists now know many plants we've called weeds are important parts of the ecology, the food web and the habitat. For example, many caterpillars eat only the leaves or flowers of what we call weeds, the caterpillars of monarch butterflies like milkweeds, tortoiseshells and peacocks love nettles. So, when we dig them up and throw those plants out, we help to cause the extinction of butterfly species ... not a good thought! Weedy annual plants like pigweed and smartweed produce a great mass of seeds and those seeds are an important food for sparrows and many other birds. Again, if we eradicate them, we help to cause extinctions. And these wild plants we call weeds are super pollen and nectar providers for bees, butterflies and all the other pollinating insects we really cannot live without. It's these pollinators that enable our food to grow. There's already a massive decline in pollinating insects, as gardeners we really should not be making things worse but trying to help Nature recover from all the damage modern farming has done.

So, begin to think more fondly of weeds and worts ... your garden, and your Planet, will be much better for it and will thank you deeply.

Veg

Veg I enjoy in the Beltane season are mainly the lovely new fresh green leaves. As I've said before I'm a salad-freak and I've always got some good leaves to eat by the 1st May. There's lots of wild foraging stuff to be had too and as I keep my hedges rough to help hedgehogs and other wildlife, they also grow some good foraging leaves as well. They're good for wildlife and good for me a win-win situation, I like that.

And seeds sown earlier will now be coming up. For me this includes peas and I do like a few fresh garden peas, despite them being pulses, and my tummy can manage a few now and again so I usually have a row of peas. I can eat them as mange-tout in salads too. Courgettes will hopefully have appeared but because the weather up here they either stay at the edge of the polytunnel where I can let them ramble outside later, or don't get transplanted outside for a while longer.

Every so often I get excited about my favourite potatoes, Pink Fir Apples, the knobbly ones, and decide to grow some that year. I'm not a big spud eater, like maybe four or five times a year, but I've always loved the taste of Pink Fir Apples although they can be difficult to grow as they get potato blight for a pastime in wet summers. If it feels promising, and the spirit of place says it'll be OK, I put in a short row of potatoes. If I have then this season is when they should be coming up. I'm not a root-eater so I don't need many.

It's also the time to beware of slugs. Warmth and moisture will bring them out in the hundreds to munch on the lettuces and pea-sproutings. If the local hedgehogs can't keep them under control, in balance – and as we've deprived hedgehogs of their habitat and killed them with slug pellets there are very few around nowadays – I have to take on the role of Apex Predator. I can't say I like it but something has to be done or they will kill a lot of plants, so I have to balance one set of deaths against another. It's certainly no time to get romantic about the whole thing! I begin my predator role by sitting with the garden spirit and getting her advice about what she feels needs doing. Then we ask the slug-spirit to come along too and the spirits of the various plant whose children are being eaten. I may take a wee while, and I tend to take a back seat, listening to what the spirits say and noting down the conclusions, then I get my orders from them. You know, it really is like being in business and going to a board meeting with all these spirits, and it can be a bit irritating as human board meetings often are. In some ways I can understand why people choose to ignore otherworld and the spirits of everything we live with … but that doesn't make ignoring them either right or a good idea! In all of life we have to do boring things sometimes, for the good of the whole, so it's great idea to get into the habit with your gardening.

It does, too, bring up a very serious human issue that gets us into lots of trouble with Nature, the Earth, and even the whole cosmos. We all have this frightful urge to be in control, in charge, and modern westernised education encourages that attitude up to the hilt. We truly are the youngest species on Planet Earth and most of the time we behave like spoilt teenagers with our control issues. If we really want to "save the Planet" we absolutely have to give all that up. As Beltane is perhaps the most explosive (think of that rocket fuel) of our Eight Seasons it's a good one to start turning over all the apple-carts of mores and morals and beliefs we've grown up with. Time to sort out the stuff that's way past its sell-by date!

So ... back to those slugs. I begin my predator job by going to the supermarket and buying a 6-pack of organic beer, not for me I must add, I don't need to get drunk to do the job! Then I go out with a torch every evening slug-hunting, those I catch go in the bucket along with a can of beer, this kills them off and, hopefully, with a not too bad death. I leave them in the bucket and in a couple of days I have the most revolting slug-n-beer soup. No, I don't eat it! I spread it around the plants I don't want the slugs to eat. And that's why I get organic beer, yes, it's more expensive than other stuff but it doesn't have anything else in it that's going to poison the soil or kill the plants. A mulch of slug soup does work too. All that telepathy-stuff I've talked about seems to provide a slug-gossip-grapevine so word gets around that my garden, lettuces, courgettes and other juicy greens are just *not* the place for a self-respecting slug with a strong self-preservation instinct to go!

Just because it's May doesn't mean we gardeners can stop worrying about soil temperature. Warming up the soil takes a while and like the old adage says, ne'er cast a clout til May be out, and that goes for sowing and planting too!

Flowers
There's one flower we pagans of all descriptions adore come May-time and that's May Blossom. The May Tree is the

Hawthorn tree, and very special to us. It's Blodeuwedd's tree, Flower Face's tree, the White Owl's tree, and a celebration of the wedding of the goddess and the god. It's a great tree to have in the garden, especially (but not only) if you can have a native hedgerow, it provides leaves, branches, shelter, food for bees from its flowers, and food for birds from the haws (that's what hawthorn berries are called). I make hawthorn jelly too, it's a delicious way to share the haws with the birds and other small creatures like dormice. Never take too much always leave some for other creatures and for the tree to seed as well. Dormice eat berries and nuts and other fruit as well as the hazelnuts they're named for and which are their main food for fattening up before hibernation. They also eat hornbeam and blackthorn fruit when hazelnuts are scarce, and they enjoy the flowers of hawthorn amongst other trees, along with the buds of young leaves, the flowers provide nectar and pollen which are super-foods for wee beasties.

Other Beltane flowers are the honeysuckle and roses. The periwinkles are out now too with that incredible blue flower. Beware Vinca major, the big periwinkle, though as that is a complete thug and will easily try to take over your whole garden. I use it in the hedges where it does an excellent job of ground cover and providing food for bees as well colour for me, and I can keep a balance there as long as I'm willing to be somewhat tough and ruthless each autumn. Wisteria will be out now and I adore the stuff although it's a bit of a pain to prune successfully. And the daisies and buttercups are coming up in the grass meadows too, I love to see that and it means the meadows are humming-alive with hungry insects as I go past.

The hardy geraniums will be flowering now too. I'm a geranium-freak, I love all the hardy varieties and am a complete sucker for them if I visit a garden centre! One of my favourites is geranium Rozanne, it begins flowering in May and keeps on going sometimes even past the first frosts. I love the tall purple pheums too, the shape of the flowers is intricately delicate and they self-seed really well so every spring I'm hunting out the latest crop and moving them if I need to because they've seeded in the middle of a path that's going to be mown. If they seed into the meadows or Prairie Bed, I leave well alone, can't have too many in those places.

I love the mulleins too. I always have some, those amazing spikes of yellow flowers reaching up into the sky with our native wild mullein and its soft furry grey leaves that harbour the caterpillars of the beautiful mullein moth. Yes, the caterpillars eat the flowers but I can share, and the moths themselves, like all moths, are magical critters. I also have some of the cultivated mulleins too, my favourites are the yellow flowers with purple centres of Verbascum (Cotswold Group) 'Gainsborough', and the white flowers with purple centres of Verbascum chaixii 'Album'. They both self-seed well too so every year I have new ones popping up in places I'd not expected.

That's another thing I'm continuously learning about as I garden – the plants know very well where it's best for them to grow, where the soil conditions are just right for them, and it's often not at all where I'd have thought of putting them! They're teaching me all the time, and I'm open to learning. I'll move beds around if I can to accommodate where the plants know they need to be – it's that not being in control thing again, I try to never know best and never know first, as I learned from CG Jung.

The cowslips are out now too, along with the last of the primroses, contrasting their pale yellows with the lovely blue of forget-me-nots. Candytuft shines white while the alliums stick up their tall heads of amazing globes of flowers of many colours, and my husband's cottage favourite, delphiniums, shimmer blue spires across the evening. I love the almost black of the purple cerinthe, the honeywort, too while Cardamine pratensis, the lady's smock or cuckoo flower, puts a shy pink-purple head out of the grasses by the pond. The snake's head fritillary and the dog's tooth violets make carpets in the shady Wolery along with the lilies of the valley that glimmer white in the evening light.

Oh … this time of year there are just so many beautiful flowers I could go on forever.

Garden Jobs

More Planning! The garden here at Bryngwyn told me in the first month after we moved in that it wanted to be a garden of the wheel of the seasons. I explored this on squared paper and offered up the ideas to the garden spirit but she firmly put me in my place by telling me to go get my compass and find out where the directions are in relation to the house.

Well blow me down with a feather, would you believe it, the front of the house faces south, the big garden at the back is on the west side, next door's paddock is on the north side while the kitchen faces due east. Sorted! That's the sides of the garden that carry the four Sun-seasons, Midwinter, Spring, Midsummer and Autumn. The four Earth/Moon seasons are the four corners, Imbolc at the north-east, Beltane at the south-east, Lammas at the south-west and Samhain at the north-west.

I had a bit of a problem with my own ideas and foibles at first. This design the garden spirit showed me meant that Lammas is in the shady semi-woody corner and I'd "expected" it would need to be hot and sunny. And Samhain would now be the place of the pond. The pond was utterly determined where it should be, right since the first day we came to view, up in the north-west corner where it's sunny for half the day and then gets shaded. Well that's all right, the sort of things a pond needs. But I was really having trouble with Lammas.

There's an old brick hut in the Lammas corner too, once upon a time it was the old privy (outside toilet) but that was long ago, it was all cleaned up and the previous person had kept her hens in there at night. I wanted to use it as a sort of cave and it very much approved of the idea so that was all OK. Some years back a stone carver friend in Scotland had made me a lovely slate sign that says The Wolery. Paul (husband) and I have a thing about Winnie the Pooh having both been brought up on the stories. Paul's family-spirit, Tylwyth as we say and totem as some other traditions call it, is the Owl, so our stone carver friend had carved a lovely Pictish owl on the slate sign too. And, we'd got a lovely barn owl model to hang up above the door to the cave.

The cave is in a little separate patch with a pair of variegated spindle bushes either side of what is obviously the entrance, and it's just the place for bluebells and shade-loving wildflowers, a tiny glade. There was old rough timber lying about so we set up a pair of posts to hold the Wolery sign to one side of the entrance and set up three other posts, all odd heights, in a slightly random group the other side. It works.

But my head was still arguing about shade being Lammas! Well why not, said the garden spirit. If it's a blazing hot August you'll need somewhere cooler to sit, somewhere that can be lush green when the meadows are sunburnt and blousy. You know you always went to places like that when you were a kid.

She was absolutely right. I remembered long summer holidays when I walked for miles down to the woods by the river and spent the day in a cool glade with dappled sunlight. How had I managed to forget those days; I'd treasured them so much at the time. So, the shady Wolery is the Lammas place in my garden.

What I'm saying here is don't get too dug into your first ideas for how your garden will be. Yes, have those initial ideas but allow the garden to show you how to modify them. You'll be surprised at how well you like the result.

And it's always good to keep your ideas fluid. Gardens are never finished, they're always a work-in-progress ... that's so much of the fun!

Celebration

Perhaps the most famous Beltane celebration in Britain is the Padstow Obby Oss. Dad first took me to see that back in 1955 when I was about seven years old. It was stunning and amazing, and just a bit scary, I remember clutching dad's hand but always trying to peer out and sometimes run out, stretching dad's arm to come with me. And what was that thing that danced? It didn't look like any horse I'd ever seen, more like a sort of dragon, and dad said yes it was, both a horse and dragon all at the same time.

By the time we'd followed the Red Oss from the Golden Lion Inn all the way up the hill, through the town, to Prideaux Place and back down again I was tired and hungry, very ready for a newspaper full of fish-n-chips as we sat on the harbour wall in the early evening. But utterly thrilled! I've been many times since and it never fails to thrill me.

The ceremony begins just before midnight on April 30th, when we gather at the Golden Lion and a woman, often the landlord's wife, calls the dead of the past year. Then we all sing the Night Song.

On May Day morning we all gather again at the Golden Lion and bring the Oss out of his stable with much laughter and lots of rude jokes. Someone begins the May Song with accordionists and drummers, and we supporters all sing along. Then the procession up through the town begins. House doors get knocked on and the Oss tries to thrust himself in – the costume is six feet wide so it just doesn't happen! – while the householder offers cake and sweets in recompense. Gifting is very much the order of the day.

At Prideaux Place the Teaser – the one who dances with the Oss – knocks on the house door and calls for the lady of the house to come down. After a bit of staged argy-bargy she does, takes the pig's bladder balloon from the Teaser and dances the Oss. Then we all go back down into the town. The whole thing takes hours!

Then there's the Maypole up in the town square, it's an

amazing sight. Children and people dance it for as long as they can keep going, lots of beer and cake and sandwiches and fish-n-chips gets consumed. It's a proper people's festival.

Beltane celebrates the union of the God and Goddess ... that's what the lady of Prideaux Place dancing the Oss is about. And all the way through the town, going up and coming down, young girls are invited under the skirts of the Oss where they'll get a quick kiss and cuddle from whoever is dancing the beast. The costume is very heavy so dancers exchange places ever twenty minutes or so.

Another way I celebrate Beltane, is to go see a good, wild Morris side. The blacked-up Silurian Morris is the wildest and from the western side of Britain through Devon and Somerset and on up through the Welsh Marches. Over the past twenty years younger Morris sides have got going and they often have their children involved in the learning too so the tradition will be carried on. And they're wild! If you get the chance go and watch a side like Beltane Morris, they'll knock your socks off! Many of the blacked up sides have dances that celebrate the union of the goddess and the god too and they're very good.

At home, I celebrate more gently with my lovely Moon Gate, in company with the candle-fire and the cup of water. I always spend time there in the evening twilight the night before May Day, browsing over the things I need to do over the season, not just in the garden but in the rest of my life too. I ask the garden spirits to help me get them in order so I can do what's most needed. On May Day morning I get up a dawn and go to the Moon Gate again, light the candle and refill the water bowl as it's likely some birds and/or beasties have needed an overnight drink. Then I stand there, in the threshold of the Moon Gate and say, "Help me do what's most needed over the next season, help me to get it right." It always works, even when at the time it doesn't look at all as I thought it would!

Midsummer Solstice

Season

Midsummer solstice is the time of the longest day and as we learned at Midwinter solstice means standstill, so again we have three days of standstill as the sun does his turnaround again. Midsummer is about the beginning of the dying of the sun. From here on we go into the darkening half of the year when the Earth works hard with the soil and the roots for next year. Meanwhile, the sun gets on with ripening all the food for the many harvests over the next few months.

Element

Air – where would we be without it? Pretty damned dead! And we have the plants to thank for so much of the oxygen we breathe. But air isn't just oxygen and it isn't just for humans either.

Air, our atmosphere, is a mixture of many gases. The most prevalent one is nitrogen and that's deadly poison to us, for instance it's what gives divers "the bends", our atmosphere is:

- Nitrogen — 78 percent.
- Oxygen — 21 percent.
- Argon — 0.93 percent.
- Carbon dioxide — 0.04 percent.
- Trace amounts of neon, helium, methane, krypton and hydrogen.
- And lots of water vapour too.

Plants use the carbon dioxide and give us oxygen in exchange. We breathe out CO_2 in exchange, along with all the other animals, so it's perfect sharing, a real lemniscate of sharing.

We each need the other, plants need animals and animals need plants. We humans are animals, we're a part of this whether we know it or not.

Altar

I always have flowers for the Midsummer altar, and there are many to choose from. As I'm a rose-freak there are always roses on my altar. As ever, I have my bowl of water and plant-pot-candle and the place of my altar in the garden is the little wildflower meadow glade I'm in process with by the south hedge.

This year, the meadow's first year, I found a little pansy flower growing up in the middle of the wild grasses. I'd certainly not seeded it there; it had come of its own accord. I took it as a sign that there was to be where I had the altar.

There's lots of stone in the garden – too much! But that will change – so I found a flat piece the right size and set it by the pansy, put my candle on water on it then went round the garden asking which roses wanted to come and be on the altar too. As I keep on saying, all it takes is the will and the courage to dare to ask, to dare to speak with the garden spirit, she or he will always answer you, all you need to do is ask and then listen for the feel of the answer. The roses who wanted to come, I could feel them calling, "Me! Me!" so I went and cut them carefully, using the secateurs for a clean cut just above a bud-node, and into the outdoor vase they went. The altar looked lovely. I found myself just sitting there in the grass, watching it, and dreaming garden-dreams that expanded into dreams for the next few months.

The south hedge has the Caradoc, my magic mountain, rising up behind it so I asked in my daydreaming what Gwyn needed of me this season. The answer came very quickly, "Climb me! Come sit in my cave." So, I did. it was the first time I'd ever climbed him so it was very special. What he told me was that I had to create a new form of the shaman training I do, online this time and using video, and that it was time my longtime friend, Fiona Dove, and I could work together. I was thrilled ... and so the Deer Trods Tribe was born.

Plants

Herbs

My list of basic culinary herbs that I always have around the garden is ...

Oregano
Thyme
Sage
Rosemary
Mint
Parsley
Garlic
Lavender
Basil
Chives
Lemon verbena
Bay tree/bush

I find I use some of at least one or two every day in cooking, and I also often take them as tisanes as they're both refreshing and rejuvenating. They're all easy to grow and I do my usual thing of mixing them up with lovely flowers as well. I'm no good at "boxes"! Nature doesn't keep things separate, one thing is always entwined and entangled with everything else, that's how nature works. We split things up as humans because it can feel too much for our brains to manage in the way nature does. That's largely because we're out of practice, we can learn to get it back.

Veg

All the fresh greens are hopefully doing well now, especially salad stuff. Young broad beans can go in the salad too, and there'll be sweet new potatoes. Like most folk I enjoy Jersey royals but I'm also very fond of the French Charlottes, they have a great texture when steamed and a lovely sweet taste that does encourage the slathering on of lots of butter!

There are so many salad veg and I grow most of them. Innumerable varieties of lettuce, my favourites are the frilly ones both green and red, young spinach is up now and the baby leaves are scrumptious, sorrel should be out, young chives, the various coloured chards that are such a stunning feast for the eyes as well as the tummy. Spring onions to spice things up along with the mustard leaves and my favourite wild rocket. If you've got young peas coming, they go well as mange tout in salads too. And the herbs like parsley, sweet cicely, mints, fennel leaves, Jack by the Hedge. I use baby kale and baby cabbage leaves, and add in weed foraging like dandelions.

And then there's the edible flowers. So many of our garden flowers that are good for the pollinators are also good for us. Pot marigolds, nasturtiums, hardy geraniums, borage flowers, lavender, thyme, oregano, pansies, rose petals, violas, poppy seeds, hollyhocks, carnations. Several have a peppery taste like nasturtiums that also has a watercress tang, and pot marigolds that are citrusy, and carnations that have a touch of cloves. Others have a nutty taste like sunflowers, viola and lavender have a sweetness while hollyhock has a marshmallow taste.

NOTE: only eat pot marigolds, calendula … African marigolds are poisonous. And only eat poppy seeds as the rest of the plant is poisonous if you ingest it.

Flowers

Midsummer, June, is *the* month for garden flowers, they put on the most wonderful show in honour of the longest day, it's quite magical.

As I'm a complete rose-freak, a disease caught from my dad

who adored them too, my midsummer garden is always awash with roses including wild roses. It's possible now to buy wild roses that have been carefully bred from seed and that's such a help to wildlife as our modern farming has killed so many of our native hedgerow plants and put our three varieties of wild rose on the danger list.

There are several different species of wild roses and their overall species is called the Dog Rose, rosa canina. It climbs up through the hedges to crown them with its lovely sweet-scented blooms that can vary in colour from white to deep pink. Whilst usually about five metres in height, Dog-rose can scramble to the tops of tall trees like a rainforest vine. Shakespeare knew it as eglantine and its simple single flowers are beloved of bees and other pollinators.

Dog-rose is the most abundant and widespread of our wild rose species and also the most variable because it's a collective of several similar subspecies. DNA suggests that the following named species are best considered as part of a single Rosa canina species complex and are therefore synonyms of Rosa canina. They are ...

R. balsamica Besser

R. caesia Sm.

R. corymbifera Borkh.

R. dumalis Bechst.

R. montana Chaix

R. stylosa Desv.

R. subcanina (Christ) Vuk.

R. subcollina (Christ) Vuk.

R. × irregularis Déségl. & Guillon

They all give bright red hips from late summer. I forage them to make rose-hip syrup, another very good winter colds preventative. Rosehip syrup made from the Dog-rose has four times the Vitamin C of blackcurrant juice and twenty times that of orange juice.

There's an old country rhyme that helps identify roses of the canina group:

> On a summer's day, in sultry weather
> Five Brethren were born together.
> Two had beards and two had none
> And the other had but half a one."

The *brethren* refers to the five sepals of the Dog-rose, two of which are whiskered on both sides, two quite smooth and the last one whiskered on one side only.

Dog-roses love the sunny side of hedgerows and will grow on a range of soils. Other names for it are wild rose, briar-rose, cat-rose, cock-bramble, hip-rose and pig-rose.

Dog roses can develop a gall, called rose bedeguar gall or Robin's pincushion. It develops as a distortion of the unopened leaf axillary or terminal buds on wild roses and is harmless. It's a growth caused by the gall wasp and is a hard woody structure with a covering of reddish-yellow, moss-like leaves. In the old days these growths were powdered and used for as a diuretic and for colic. As a child I remember Mrs Webber next door asking us to collect them and then showing us how to make them into amulets to hang around our necks against whooping-cough. I never got whooping cough, nor did the other two girls, or their brothers, who made and wore the amulets although several other children in the village did.

Garden Jobs

Bee Magic is what comes to mind for me at midsummer. Bees feature in folklore and magic all around the world, while both honey and bee venom are used in many different traditions.

Bees help all other living things by pollinating plants and so maintaining everyone's food supply, not just ours but all living creatures including the plants themselves. If we're careful and not greedy, and ask before we take, bees give us humans honey and beeswax. Honey is one of the most delicious things nature (and the bees) gives us, it's very easy for humans to get addicted to it and so harm bees in the way they work with them. Honey was always considered a precious, special and sacred thing, not something to always go in the weekly shop at the supermarket. That whole attitude comes of a complete disrespect for bees and the whole of the natural world – humans need to change that.

One of the old stories by Uncle Perce used to tell me of the bees was what's known round the world as "go tell the bees". It's not just about deaths although that's the one that's known best nowadays but about everything in life, in the lives of the people where the bees have their home.

Uncle Perce was an amazing beekeeper. I've seen him climb a ladder into a holly tree and take a swarm of bees in his hands, carefully climb back down again, still holding the bundle of bees and take them to an empty hive. Some bees would be buzzing round his head, and he got the occasional sting, but he was never hurt by them and he never hurt the bees either. He always went to talk with the bees every day, the hives were in his half-acre of orchard along with the hens, so he'd stop by the hives and tell the bees how the day had been. One of my pocket-money jobs was to feed the hens in the evening, collect the eggs and put them to bed in the big wheeled hen-houses. Those houses were like the shepherd's huts people go glamping in nowadays, except the wheels weren't so tall, and as a wee kiddie I always wanted one to live in but they were always full of hens! And Uncle Perce taught me to talk with the bees too as I went on my hen-rounds of an evening.

I'm still nervous of bees so I don't keep them in the ordinary way but my friend Julie next door is making me a log-hive so I will keep bees but I won't be taking any honey from them. I'd love to give them a home in my garden – although they already make their own homes here as the place is always a-buzz with bees. But when I have a log-hive I can go sit-with them again ...

Moon Gardens

Midsummer moon, indeed all the moons, have a fascination for most pagans and many other folk as well. I'm planning next year to grow a part of the garden as a Moon Garden.

There are lots of night-blooming flowers and these are very good for moths. They also provide a beautiful and fragrant backdrop for when I sit out of a summer night, perhaps doing a ritual or perhaps just sitting-with the garden spirit, Gwyn ap Nudd over in his mountain, and all the nature spirits of the garden too.

Sitting out of a summer evening also helps me get to know all the night-denizens who I share this place with ... like the bats, I think we have two sorts but I'm no bat expert it's just they look different as I watch them. They live in our attic space, in the roof, so we're a special site and people can't, it's illegal as bats are a protected species, do any changes to the house without checking about the bats, I'm really pleased about that.

Night Blooming plants include ...

The fragrance of sweet rocket is as good as a violet's, and most pronounced in the evening. It's a biennial, and comes in pink and white forms, and self-seeds readily around the garden so once I've sown it all I need do is watch where it's chosen to come up this year.

Nicotiana sylvestris, the woodland tobacco plant (that's what sylvestris means), is tall and has elegant, long, white flowers with an intense fragrance, especially in the evening. It's another biennial or short-lived perennial that self-seeds readily.

Night phlox is a neatly domed, compact evergreen plant that is smothered with pretty, white scented flowers in summer.

It's not reliably hardy though so I'll need to sow it each year. If I keep deadheading it then it'll go on flowering for ages. Its flowers open up at dusk and have a fragrance reminiscent of honey or vanilla.

I love wisteria and many of them are scented, Wisteria floribunda cultivars being the best with strongest scent at night. I may put it over the Moon Gate (very appropriate for a moon garden!) and see if will reach over to the house wall there too.

From midsummer the star jasmine or Trachelospermum jasminoides has pretty white fragrant flowers. It's an evergreen climber but only borderline hardy so I don't know yet what the garden spirit will say about this. I'd like one but if she says no ... well there's no point in me trying then as I know the poor thing will only die and that's not fair to it.

I've got lots of our native honeysuckle, Lonicera periclymenum, and some growing up the Moon Gate already. I'll put some more into the hedge and maybe rambling around the coppiced willow as well. Its scent gets stronger into the evening.

Night-scented stock is an easy-to-grow annual that insects love while its tiny blooms pack a really fragrant punch. If I sow it in July it'll mean lots of moon garden scent and blossoms for late summer.

I've got pinks in the garden already but not where I'd like the moon garden. All it needs is to divide and then I can move some next spring. It's a lovely, low-growing perennial with silver leaves and mine has pink, clove-scented blooms.

Phlox paniculata, the border phlox, is a good compact herbaceous perennial and perfect for the moon garden.

I can't grow Moonflower in my cool-temperate climate but I can grow one of its relations, Morning Glory, it can get up to eight feet long and the open flowers are around 5-6" in diameter. Impressive! They're not really hardy here but I can at least sow the seeds every year and maybe some will be able to manage a winter sometimes.

I already have Evening Primrose, love its tall stately habit and it self-seeds well so I just need to ask if it can handle growing where I'd like it to – fingers crossed. It can be a bit of a thug so I always need to check each spring just how many seedlings it's given me. It gives off its scent at dusk, the twilight when the Faer Folk come out.

I'm also going to add some of my favourite silvery plants, to give me more of a moon-feel, like artemisia, lavender, curry plant, cineraria. The deeply-cut, silver-grey foliage of this is very lovely, but it's a half-hardy perennial that's best grown as a half-hardy annual and easy to grow from seed. I'd like Senecio 'Angel Wings' too and that's a hardy evergreen shrub that makes good ground cover and shelter for wee beasties so will do well here.

Silver Thyme is another favourite and you just can't have too much thyme (time – chuckle!) in the garden. It's fragrant lemon-scented leaves are edged with silver and its flowers are a pale silvery-lavender.

Lamb's Ears are another must and so easy to grow as well as being yet another plant for the pollinators. They have furry, pale greenish-silvery-grey leaves sort of like a lamb's ear, and can also be a bit of a thug so I'll need to keep a check on seedlings here too!

Mugwort I already have and love dearly, I use it as a tisane for dreaming-sleep. Its silvery-green leaves smell amazing.

Silver Sage, I'd like to grow this but it will be another possibly difficult one so I need to ask the garden spirit if she'd like it and if the garden can manage it. Silver sage, salvia argentea, is a biennial or short-lived Mediterranean perennial so British winters may well be too wet for it. Its silvery-woolly leaves form a fury rosette and it has erect stems of bluish-white flowers in late summer but often dies after it's flowered. We'll have to see what garden spirit says.

And I have an old coppiced willow that stands to one corner of the area I'm thinking of, another silvery plant. I'll go sit-with her and see what she has to say about the idea and what suggestions she has for me with regard to planting ... and ask her if she'd like to twine with the wisteria. Fingers crossed!

Celebration: Longest Day

The summer solstice in the Northern Hemisphere falls on 21st June. As with Midwinter, Midsummer signals the turning of the year again as the sun reaches his climax, the highest point of his arc, and prepares to go down again into the darkness of the Earth's womb. Now, the nights begin to grow longer each day as the sun's arc gets lower in the sky. So, while modern people tend to celebrate the longest day for its light, pagans also celebrate the beginning of the coming darkness. It's something of a farewell feast for the light and a welcoming feast for the dark.

Midsummer night – as Shakespeare tells in his play – is a time of dreams, a time when dreams can come true. If we have a special wish, we take it into our dreams.

A ritual I use for this is to light a midsummer celebration fire – I do so enjoy working with fire! – as twilight comes on and sit beside the fire pondering on and sitting-with my wish. I ask the wish to show itself to me as clearly as possible – this can take some time – and I doodle-draw my impressions of this, that helps me to be as clear as possible about what I'm wishing for. When I'm as clear as I feel I can be I write the wish on another piece of paper, fold it four times and set it into the fire with the words, "Summer Sun, hear my wish, bring me a dream to show me how to bring the wish to life." I find it works, some of my most important wishes, like about moving home, have come about successfully very soon after me doing this Midsummer ritual.

Lammas

Season

Lammas, August 1, is the first harvest festival on the Pagan calendar. Like many of our festivals it's related to the old agricultural holiday celebrating the reaping of grain. The word Lammas probably comes from the Old English words for "loaf mass" as freshly baked loaves of bread would be prepared from the first grain, and the first ale of the new season made, to feast the gods and thank them for the harvest. It's also called Lughnasadh in Gaelic, after Lugh who is the Sun god in Gaelic lands.

In Britain it's the feast of John Barleycorn – our old name for the god who dies each year at the first harvest in order to give his blood and seed to the land for next year's grain. The bread of his body is eaten as the loaves from the new harvest. Lammas is a time of death and rebirth, all things die and all things are reborn again in their season, something all pagans know ... and pagan gardeners know it very well as we see it happen in our gardens year on year.

Element

Like the other Earth/Moon festivals of our year, Lammas combines two elements, this time Fire and Air. These two go well together, the more air a fire gets the faster and hotter it burns, all firemen know and fear that, partly why the tell us not to open doors in case the extra air from the open door causes a monumental flare.

Altar

My altar for Lammas is actually on the shadiest part of the garden, the Wolery, which is my woodland patch. It's a little glade that, in spring is full of bluebells, primroses, lilies of the valley, snowdrops and native daffodils. The holly hedge grows high there, the little ivy-covered hut in the corner invites secrets, the owl-figure who hangs above the hut door whispers magic. A friend who's a craftswoman is going to make me a metal firepit for in the glade and I'm slowly collecting log seats so we can sit there of a Lammas evening and have our own barbecue feast.

That was not yet ready to do this year so what I did instead was make a small fire from some of the hedge prunings – using our own wood – and celebrate the first harvest festival with homemade nut-flour bread, some local cheese and a glass of local ale. It was good. And I felt really good as it's also the first anniversary of being in this house, with this spirit of place. Be sure I thanked her deeply and the spirit of these hills, Gwyn ap Nudd, who brought us here.

Plants

Herbs

Meadowsweet – also known as Queen-Of-The-Meadow, Bridewort and Bride of the Meadow, is one of my favourite herbs. I adore its scent and the creamy-white billowing flowers always make me think of fairy bridal gowns. It was indeed a traditional herb for circlets and bouquets for weddings at this time of year. The Druids wore it as a garland for Lammas celebrations and it was a staple for the old wives' love spells. Its heady scent cheers the heart.

Mint – is another of the three herbs the Druids revered. I love it and use it for all sorts of things. The bees love it too and my mint patches are always buzzing like fury when the flowers are out. At this time of year, with good new potatoes, peas and lamb, mint is an absolute must for the kitchen.

Vervain – is the third of the Druids' herbs. It's also known as verbena, Verbena officinalis, and a perennial herb native to

Europe and Asia. Its beautiful silky purple flowers always entrance me, and it's another one the bees love.

Calendula – I always have calendula in the garden, it has so many uses – ground cover, in salads, as companion planting in the vegetable-pottager, and an excellent calming and sleep inducing herb. It's another of my favoured sun flowers along with dandelion.

Veg

Oh, there's so much available from the veg patch at Lammas, depending on what you've sown of course. Tomatoes, cucumbers and aubergines should be coming out of the polytunnel now, and maybe outdoor tomatoes and cucumbers too depending on the weather. Main crop carrots will be taking over from the early ones. All your beans should be going like the clappers now too. Fortunately, beans, if blanched, freeze well so the usual glut of beans can be easily stored in the freezer for winter treats.

Artichokes and potatoes will be ready now, and if you have a plum tree that is hopefully bearing well. The first beetroots should be good for picking now and there's likely some baby beets for salad too. I'm usually up to my ears in lettuce and salad now, so I keep wondering every year if I'll end up with ears like Peter Rabbit from all the salad greens I eat!

I keep sowing salad every week now to make sure I've got lettuce and salad leaves to pick over the winter too. The soil needs to stay warm is seeds are to germinate now the days are getting shorter. Of course, the plants know this so their ancient instincts tell them either to slow down ready for a winter sleep or hurry up because they feel they've not reproduced yet. if you do cut-n-come-again with your salad greens as I do then the latter will be true for your plants. As you keep cutting so you stop the reproduction works (i.e. bolting and seeding) getting under way.

If you like winter greens like late cabbages and broccoli then now's about your last chance to sow them in the ground, so get on with that if it's what you enjoy.

And for the wild foraging ... blackberries, hedgefuls of them hopefully. I make jam, juice for winter treats and to keep cold viruses away, and cordials for a taste of summer at midwinter in a kir made with sparkling wine. And then there's blissful blackberry and apple pies. I make these using chestnut flour as I can't eat grains and the pastry can be just as good, in fact – because of how very tasty chestnut flour is – I think even better!

It really is harvest time. From the penury of late winter, we've now transformed, six months later, to the cornucopia of the harvest. Plenty to celebrate here.

Flowers

Like the veg, the flowers will probably be glutting over lots of the garden, giving the warm summer bees some of their best feeds of the year. I love repeat-flowering roses and these are coming into their own again around Lammas so my garden is full of various rose scents. Lavender, catmint, curry plant, and wormwood, the silver-leaved herbs, are all scenting the garden up too and they go so well with the roses.

The fuchsias are in full swing now too. I first met them in gardens on the North Devon coast when I was about eight and fell in love. My last garden wouldn't grow them well but they love this garden, this autumn I'm plant a hedgeful of hardy fuchsia, including the lovely white one, Hawkshead, around the back of the pond.

The sedums, stonecrops, do well at this season too. I've got some climbing around the pebbles and rocks by the pond, some at the edge of the herb bed creeping onto the path, and some climbing over the brick edge of the bed by the tank pond at the front.

It's the time for scabious and all the big daisy plants of the meadows too, and the first asters. Asters are really helpful for insects because they flower late and keep going into late autumn or early winter, so late bees and insects can find food. All the knapweeds (centaurea) are doing well too, and the achillea, and the hyssops. It's a time of plenty to help the insects and small beasties get ready for winter.

Garden Jobs

This garden jobs section is longer than the others because it's a time when I can get going with preparation for new veg and fruit beds next year. For me, Lammas means lots of clearing of weeds – plants in the wrong place! But I try not to be too enthusiastic as the soil doesn't like being bare, that's why it grows what we call worts and weeds, herbs to help cover itself up so the moisture doesn't leak out as the sun gets going at full strength. But we will have needed to give some air to our vegetables, and make space for the rain to permeate through the leaves so it reaches the soil and so the roots of the plants. Just don't get too carried away!

But the weeding will have given you good piles of green matter to compost and Lammas is certainly a time for this. Composting resembles the life-death-life cycle enacted in the John Barleycorn dances and songs, we cut down and dig up, the plants who are too lusty, or that we don't want in that place, and put them in the compost bin. We do similar as we harvest too, pulling the holms of the peas up but leaving the roots with their nitrogen nodules in the soil to help it. We take and eat the last of the peas but the holms go in the compost too, as they're dryer than many of the weeds we pull up they help even up the greens and the browns. Same goes for the beans, but many of these like runner beans will still be flowering and fruiting at Lammas. The early, and maybe some of the mid-season, potatoes will be ready to dig though and, again, their tops will all go in the bin. So, we really do follow John Barleycorn in our gardens.

Composting in Small Gardens

I got this idea from the Permaculture folk, Mak Tully, to be precise. As he rightly says, not that many people have acres of land, it's only a dream, and a lot of people find the quarter-acre I garden a scary size to manage. And compost bins do take up space; I've got seven 300L Rotol Compost Converters and I love them but each one takes up one square metre of space on the ground. They do smaller ones, and you don't need seven for the average town garden, but it's still a lot of ground space to take up. Lots of people find the "green daleks" ugly, don't want to look at them when they're out in the garden, so they hide them in a dark corner somewhere which is completely useless for making compost. Compost needs heat to do well so bins need a sunny spot ... probably just where you want to sit and enjoy the beauty of your garden!

On the pagan principle of harming none if at all possible, we often use a lot of permaculture ideas and this one I've found to work well. Instead of one big compost bin, Mak suggests having lots of smaller ones set around the garden in places where you want to grow vegetables or other plants that are going to be dug up for whatever reason. You're going to dig a hole, bury a cardboard box in it then fill it with stuff from your kitchen caddy or weeds you take up, even add a wee bit of grass mowings. Then you bury the box.

So first, collect yourself some reasonable size cardboard boxes – we all get these and often don't know what to do with them! Lower sided boxes about 25-40cm deep I find the easiest. Now, decide where you want to bury the box. The veg plot is often the best but if you want to make a new bed for flowers of herbs, or plant a tree or shrub, that works well too.

When you've chosen the place, dig a hole big enough to fit a cardboard box in. Remove the soil that came out of the hole, and put in a tub or bag as you'll be using this later on in a couple of weeks or so. Put the box into the hole and make lots of holes in the base of the box, I usually stab it with the fork a good few times to do this.

I try to pick a time to dig the hole when my kitchen caddy is needing to be emptied so I can do that straight into the box and set the process off immediately. I keep emptying the kitchen caddy and weeds into the box until it's full, adding some "browns" as I do along like dry leaves, ripped up paper as long as it's not shiny or otherwise treated or chemically enhanced and ripped up egg boxes. Keep the proportions of greens and browns about half and half. I also try to layer it so greens and browns are 50/50. Mak says in his advice to mix it all up but I've got three fractures in my spine, rheumatoid arthritis and osteoporosis – in other words I hurt a lot! – so I try to save myself effort when I can.

When the bottom of the box is covered with compostable stuff get the soil you took out to make the hole and put a layer of soil over the stuff in the box so it's covered completely – but don't fill the box up. Then water it. Over the next few weeks, keep adding layers of kitchen caddy and weeds, cover each layer with soil and water it, until the layers reach the top of the box. When it's full and ground level again leave it alone for 2-4 weeks, allowing the bugs and insects and worms to do their work.

So, a month from the time the hole is full to the top again your box will be ready for planting. The soil you just made in the composting process will be nice and rich, lots of food for whatever you want to grow there. I've used this method to start a rhubarb bed, for planting raspberry canes, new flower beds, and any/everywhere in the veg garden. The method works particularly well for any plants that are greedy feeders but do remember that not all plants are. Check what they need before you get started, you can kill plants by overfeeding just as easily as underfeeding so take care and learn about the plants.

If you think about it, this is a more sort of neat-n-tidy way of doing just what nature does. Leaves, fall, plants die, their dead bodies lie on the land and the animals, birds, bugs and beasties come and do their magic with the dead stuff. And it all goes back to being soil again, new things grow. Life comes forth from death, just as John Barleycorn tells us.

Hügelkultur

As we're on the Lammas subject of life-out-of-death let's go into Hügelkultur as it's really useful and interesting. You can do it on a small scale as well as in a big way too. Hügelkultur are no-dig raised beds with a difference. They hold moisture, build fertility, maximise surface volume and are great spaces for growing fruit, vegetables and herbs, all of which I love eating and using.

The box-composting we just talked about is another form of Hügelkultur, pronounced *Hoo-gul-culture*, the word means *hill culture* or *hill mound* but in this case, we're digging it in, digging pits, rather than mounding it up. Or perhaps what's called Lasagne Gardening, I'll talk about that after Hügelkultur.

Hügelkultur uses all the waste stuff from the garden, really eco-friendly. Instead of putting branches, leaves and grass clippings in bags out for the bin men you use them to build a hugel bed. Building a hugel bed has lots of ecological advantages and helps the gardener. For a start, the wood you lay at the bottom decays gradually – as it does in nature – and so provides a consistent source of long-term nutrients for the plants, a large bed could give out a constant supply of nutrients for 20 years, or even longer if you use only hardwoods. Most of us can't do that as we have a mixture of trees in our gardens and hedges, and it's their prunings that will go to be the bottom of our hügelkultur bed. The composting wood also generates heat and that can extend the growing season for that bed; we all know seeds don't germinate unless the soil temperature is just right. Plants are so clever, they know, just know, exactly when the temperature is right for them to sprout, and each plant is slightly different – I find that stunning.

Then the wood at the bottom helps soil aeration enormously,

as those branches and logs break down, they will reform themselves, with the aid of the bugs, into good soil that allows air as well as moisture through so the plants can breathe. Your hügelkultur bed will be long term no-till, and as I'm somewhat crippled, as I said above, that suits me down to the socks.

And the logs, branches and twigs act like a sponge. They soak up and store rainwater then, especially with the aid of the mycorrhiza, they release during the drier times. You may never need to water your hugel bed again after the first year unless there's a really long-term drought. Another ecological advantage is that the wood sequesters carbon into the soil.

So, what do you do? The process is really simple, you mound logs, branches, leaves, grass clippings, straw, cardboard, petroleum-free newspaper, manure, compost or whatever other biomass you have available, top the mound with soil and plant your veggies.

Sounds almost too good to be true, doesn't it? But it isn't, and it really does all those things. If you want to start by using a part of your lawn then Hügelkultur expert, Sepp Holzer, advises skimming off to a depth of 10 cm and put it to one side as you'll use it again soon. Dig a 30cm deep trench as wide as you want the bottom of the bed, and fill it with logs and branches. A good time to do this is when you're just about to trim the hedge and maybe prune some of the trees.

Now, cover the logs with the upside-down turf. On top of the turf add grass clippings, seaweed, compost, aged manure, straw, green leaves, mulch, etc. It'll take a wee while to do this as you need to collect the material but start immediately and keep adding as you have the material.

Sepp Holzer likes steep hugel beds, he says it avoids compaction of the soil underneath and I can see his point, the soil under the walls of your house will be very compacted from carrying the weight of the house wall. A narrower hugel bed means, over time, less of soil underneath suffers from the increased pressure. Another advantage is that steep beds mean more surface area in your garden for plants, and the height makes easy harvesting, especially for folks as can't bend to well like me. And the greater the mass, the greater the water-retention benefits. If you put fresh grass clippings or green leaves – nitrogen-rich material – right on the wood it helps jump start the composting process. Seaweed, straw, dead leaves, leaf mould, kitchen caddy stuff all help too.

It's a lot slower than the cardboard box gardening we began with. During the first year, as the wood begins to break down both it and the fungi use a lot of the nitrogen from out of the surrounding environment, including compost materials you just put around it, in its breakdown process. Some people call this stealing but it's not, the nitrogen provides the energy that fuels the breakdown, without it nothing would happen, there'd be no composting and so no making of soil. To plant the hugel bed in its first year you need to add more nitrogen still so the plants you want to grow also have enough to eat to enable them to do the job. As ever, it's all exchange, you give and so you receive, you receive and you give back in return. I plant species that have a minimal nitrogen requirement to help this along, things like swede, turnip, chicory, asparagus, aubergine, lettuce, garlic, onion, squash, pepper, tomato and sweet corn. You can see that gives you quite a wide choice of things to grow while, peas for instance, actually give back nitrogen and so will help the hugel bed grow. Once the wood absorbs nitrogen to its fill, the wood will start to break down and start to give nitrogen back in the process. In the end you will be left with a beautiful bed of nutrient rich soil.

What sorts of wood work best in hügelkultur? Hardwoods like oak, ash, beech, birch, elm, rowan, holly, hazel, hawthorn, the trees of our native hedgerows, have broad leaves, produce a fruit or nut, and often go dormant losing their leaves in winter. Their wood contains cells that conduct water, as well as tightly packed, thick fibre cells. Softwoods like fir, pine, larch, yew, juniper, have needles, and their water-conducting cells are not the dense wood fibre cells that hardwoods have. So, the hardwoods break down slowly and so your hardwood hugel bed will last longer, hold water for more years and add nutrients for more years than softwood ones. But softwoods will work well too if not for so long as the softwood bed will just disintegrate quicker. Mixing woods with softwoods and branches on top, to give off nutrients first, and hardwoods on bottom, will work well if you can get both types of wood. Don't forget though, the newly decomposing softwoods at the top will need to eat up a lot of nitrogen at first, so compensate for that.

Lasagne Gardening

Another no-dig method I sometimes use and find works well is Lasagne Gardening.

This is a no-dig, no-till organic gardening method that results in rich, fluffy soil with very little work from the gardener.[1] The name «lasagne gardening" has nothing to do with what you'll be growing in the garden. Instead, it refers to the method of building the garden: adding layers of organic materials that will "cook down" over time, resulting in nutrient-rich soil that will help your plants thrive. Also known as sheet composting, Lasagne Gardening is beneficial for the environment because you're turning old household waste like cardboard and paper that you'd otherwise send to the rubbish into organic soil. You add kitchen scraps and all the other things you put in the compost bin too. It will all turn into good stuff to grow new plants in.

The basic idea is to cut down the large weeds and then spread a thick mat of cardboard over them, I peg it down too as we do get gales up here. Then soak it well with the hosepipe as that will help it rot down more quickly and begin layering. Everything goes into it, leaves, grass clippings, rotted manure and ordinary garden compost are the *meat* layers then add more cardboard for the next pasta layer. Do this for several layers and finish with a topping of soaked cardboard.

Some people say you can plant straight into your lasagne but, like with the hügelkultur there's a lot of nitrogen lock-up so you need to think about what you sow in there at first. The nitrogen lockup – i.e. the nitrogen not being available to the plants you want to grow – happens because the cardboard is carbon-rich, like the hügelkultur wood, and so needs the nitrogen to begin the decomposition process. Adding lots of lawn-mowings really helps this along as they're nitrogen-rich. The lawn-mowings also help the plants you sow into the lasagne bed so it's quite a reasonable win-win situation.

If you want to use the bed for perennial plants it will certainly work and you can plant into it pretty quickly. Things like soft fruit, rhubarb, even apples, pears and cherries should do well. I always add extra muck around the roots and some soil from the compost heap as I plant them to help them along. The wet cardboard is easy to dig into but as the lasagne layers are semi-rotted so it's essential to make sure the plant has enough soil around the roots to hold its own. Once it's established it'll send new roots to explore and so anchor itself more strongly. I also add a watering pipe tin amongst the tree roots "just in case" but the soil is so rich, so quickly, I've not yet had to use it. Runner beans and tomatoes love the rich, semi-rotting soil too and grow well.

The first year I tried it I had a bit of a dig after a few months and was amazed to find about 90% of the weeds were gone ... and with no broken back! As I've got three crush-fractures in my spine and a cracked rib that was a total blessing. The soil in the lasagne bed was very quickly rich with life, full of fat, wiggling worms of all sizes, so of all generations and that's a really good sign. It was so much better than the bed I'd dug at the expense of my back! The soil beautiful, dark, and crumbly, it's a joy to look at and feels really good in your hands. I'm doing more of this sort of gardening now, just love this soil.

Celebration: John Barleycorn

Morris sides dance the John Barleycorn Dance at these festivals, it's like a play danced to the pulsing rhythms of the side's band. I've been to many such celebrations, often with big crowds, and everyone is tapping and stamping their feet, the music and the dancing are as hypnotic and entrancing as a drum circle. Indeed, when and where I was brought up the Morris side was a part of our rituals and nowadays that's coming back as more and more people want it.

In the John Barleycorn dance the dancers wear colours linked with the four elements John Barleycorn needs to live and grow:

- EARTH - Green/Brown
- AIR - Yellow/White
- FIRE - Red
- WATER – Blue

Often the dancers' costumes are made partly of straw and John Barleycorn wears sheaves of corn in his hat or a crown made of them. I remember making corn dollies at primary school in preparation for the festival. We children carried them and held them round the dancing circle.

John Barleycorn invokes these elements and then the dance begins. It culminates when John Barleycorn, now full grown, is slain to provide the harvest and the blood to fertilise the ground for the coming year. In the dance, he's then revived to show the cycle of death and rebirth beginning once again. In our festivals he is reborn at Midwinter, the time of Sun Return, then at Imbolc the corn dollies are buried in the first furrow ploughed.

Here's the words of John Barleycorn's song, and you can hear it sung by many good bands and singers on YouTube.

There were three men come out of the west, their fortunes for
to try
And these three men made a solemn vow, John Barleycorn
would die
They've ploughed, they've sown, they've harrowed, thrown
clods upon his head
Till these three men were satisfied John Barleycorn was dead

They've let him lie for a very long time till the rains from
heaven did fall
And little Sir John sprang up his head and so amazed them all
They've let him stand till midsummer's day and he looks
both pale and wan
Then little Sir John's grown a long long beard and so become
a man

They've hired men with the sharp-edged scythes to cut him
off at the knee
They've rolled him and tied him around the waist, treated
him most barbarously
They've hired men with the sharp-edged forks to prick him
to the heart
And the loader has served him worse than that for he's bound
him to the cart

So they've wheeled him around and around the field till
they've come unto a barn
And here they've kept their solemn word concerning
Barleycorn
They've hired men with the crab tree sticks to split him skin
from bone
And the miller has served him worse than that for he's ground
him between two stones

There's beer all in the barrel and brandy in the glass
But little Sir John, with his nut-brown bowl, proved the
strongest man at last

Harvesting the Land

So, Lammas is all about harvesting the land. That's harvesting
what the land gives us and, at the same time, giving back to the
Earth in exchange for the bounty she's given us. The pagan way
of life is all about exchange, giving as well as taking, replenishing
but not hoarding, and it's a great way to garden too.

Autumn Equinox

Season

Equinoxes are amazing times and happen twice in the year, first at spring then at autumn, the second day in the year when there's equal dark and light. From spring to autumn, remember, there is more light than dark each day then, from autumn to spring, there is more darkness than light each day.

As we've said, plants are incredibly sensitive to light and can tell how much there is each day as well as its quality and strength. They time their own inner processes of growth and die-back, sprouting seeds or letting them lie dormant, leaf-shedding or producing, making buds, flowering and fruiting, in accordance with the amount and strength of the light from the sun.

The gardener who understands about this is far better placed to work well with her plants, and her soil, than one who is following the book by rote. As my plantsman teacher, Duncan Coombes, at Pershore used to say, "the plant hasn't read the book!" – very true Duncan, so it's seriously silly of us humans to expect them to perform by the book. The movement of the sun, its arcs, how low or high it is in the sky, the times of year, these are all intrinsic parts of being pagan; we grow up with these things, they inform our way of life and we get know them in our bones, so they're also a core part of pagan gardening.

Solstices, equinoxes, indeed the whole Earth-Sun process, happens for huge and vital cosmic reasons. No, I'm not exaggerating, they really are cosmic. Our home planet is a part of the whole cosmos, in the path she makes around the sun. It's actually fun to read up on this and YouTube has some super videos that *show* you what happens rather than just trying to read it all in scientific language which is usually fairly brain-scrambling at best to those of us not trained that way.

These cosmic events, the equinoxes, have an enormous effect

on plants and animals, and so on gardening, twice every year. There's a thing called the solar window. Between 9.00 a.m. and 3.00 p.m. the Earth receives the maximum amount of energy from the sun and plants know this and respond to it. Have you watched flowers close up earlier and earlier each day as we head through autumn and into winter? Or even before that as there comes to be less and less light each day from Midsummer on. Water lilies show it very well; I love watching them open as I sit beside the pond with my morning coffee, then again, I watch them close as I sit there with my afternoon tea. They're good moments to sit-with in between work, and we all need to sit-with stuff as well as slogging on with it; Those moments of *sitting-with* take you out of yourself so you can see and hear the natural world around you, and so get more perspective. Gardeners need that – you can't work well with plants and soil unless you learn to listen, watch, hear, observe, and understand what's going on with them.

The lilies I enjoy watching are responding to that solar window. They know instantly the moment it closes for them in their pond, and when it opens again the next morning. They open their flowers to the sun, giving off their amazing light-colours way beyond the visual spectrum we humans can see. But it's all in the range the insects use, so the lilies offer up their pollen as food in exchange for the insects taking that pollen to inseminate another plant. Round and round goes the cycle, pollen arriving from another plant so they can produce their seeds, and gifting pollen to the next plant the bee will visit. Yet again, everything in the natural world is exchange and pagan gardeners know that, work with it.

That solar window gets bigger each day between the midwinter and midsummer, then smaller every day between midsummer and midwinter. The equinoxes are the tipping points, and very significant for gardeners.

Element

Fire

"Tyger, tyger, burning bright." I'm reminded of William Blake's old poem.

> Tyger Tyger, burning bright,
> In the forests of the night;
> What immortal hand or eye,
> Could frame thy fearful symmetry?

It really speaks to me of the something else that we know in our bones in the old ways.

Fire is incredible stuff as I've said before. It transmutes matter right back to its component atoms so they're all ready to make themselves into a new form ... cabbages to kings, to misquote the Walrus in Alice in Wonderland. Sun-fire has worked with Earth-fire to make atoms into yummy vegetables we love to eat.

Altar

A fire altar opens up so many possibilities for us. Just about everyone enjoys fire; a roaring fire in the hearth, the fire in the woodburner, a campfire under the stars. I always make my autumn altar a fire altar and at the centre will be a living fire so I can sit out – well wrapped up if it's cold – and watch what we wildcampers call Bush TV, watch the dancing of the flames.

Flame-colours are wonderful, they go through the rainbow too but they're different from the colours of water in sunlight, partly because flames create their own light, they don't need the sun to shine. Ever since I was a child, I've called it *shining darkly*, does that give you a feel of it? Flame colours have an almost metallic sheen. They're fierce and wild to me yet they give me warmth and cook my food. Flames are my dark shining friends.

Plants
Herbs

Autumn herbs for me are heavily about elderberries. These wonderful things are an ancient and effective remedy, and preventative, for the many cold and flu viruses that come over the winter time. Making elderberry cordial is not at all hard and a lovely scented job for rainy days; you can easily find recipes via Google.

The other thing I do, have probably been doing over the summer, is drying herbs from the garden so I have them to use over the winter. Again, it's not hard, just hang them in bunches upside-down and let them dry naturally. I stick a brown paper bag over the head if they're full of seed so I catch those too, the seeds will naturally fall out as the herb dries, that's part of how they spread their seed.

Second harvest is often a time I make herb tinctures too. Again, that's not difficult and you can get recipes and how-to through Google. Herbs can help keep us healthy as well as help heal diseases, preventative, and isn't it better not to have some illness than to let it happen when you could have prevented it? I think so. And many herb tinctures are good at this.

Veg

It's harvest, again, so there's loads of choice. Likely you can get most of the veggies you love nice and fresh at this time. But it's also a good idea to freeze those you can so you have food for the leaner winter months. Many veg will freeze successfully, they usually need blanching first – dunking in boiling water for a moment or two, no longer, the ideas isn't to cook them but just slightly adjust their chemistry so they hold their colour and taste well in the freezing process.

Refrigeration is one of the modern technologies I really do appreciate. I'm by no means a Luddite smashing all modern technology, I'm just very selective and use what really works for me. I like laptops and mobile phones too! But I'm seriously not into processed food, and I use my car as little as possible; living out in the wilds, a quarter of a mile up a farm track with grass growing down the middle of it, that leads into a single track lane for three miles before you get to a "proper road" I don't live without a car. And I'm crippled, can't walk far and certainly can't use a bicycle, nor can I carry shopping bags either, so car it is. But I'm careful, use it when I need and don't go jauntering around for no purpose. However, purpose does include meeting a friend on the Long Mynd or Wenlock Edge for a walk. Delights, like being deep in nature, are what feeds my soul, and soul-feeding is a big part of gardening too.

Nuts

Autumn is the second harvest so yet more things come to fruit, more apples, the last of the pears, and nuts from the woods. I love nuts, use them a lot in cooking, seeds too.

Most places I've lived have a sweet chestnut forest near enough for me to walk in so I've always collected chestnuts and then used them in cooking, I love the taste. I use chestnut flour a lot for bread, cakes, pastry but it's too hard for me to grind them up to make my own flour unfortunately. You can use chestnuts in all sorts of cooking though, get experimental and give it a go.

I'm especially gifted here as there's a lovely old chestnut tree at the end of our track where it meets the lane. In autumn I go down there and collect as many chestnuts as I can store,

I collect hazel nuts too, when I can get in ahead of the squirrel! I don't object to Ms Squirrel taking them though, they're her natural larder and I can get food in other ways she can't. And I certainly don't object to the dormice having them, coiled in a ball asleep, dormice are one of the cutest creatures on the planet.

When I was younger and fitter, I used to collect acorns too, and grind them up. But acorn require a lot of processing – look it up on Google – and I no longer have the time nor energy for that.

In my last garden, back in Herefordshire, we had a walnut tree, I love walnuts and always collected as many as I could. This walnut was old and tall and I'm no longer a tree climber so I ended up working a game with the local squirrels. I'd tease them and they'd literally throw the nuts at me! I got hit quite often but it's not the end of the world, hardly a bruise and it did serve me right for teasing the squirrels ... and it did mean I got fresh-picked nuts to save. When they've been lying on the ground, they begin their process of rotting their hard outer shell so the seed can escape, wriggle its way into the soil and begin growing so of course they don't taste so good.

Flowers

Autumn has some wonderful flowers, beautiful colours that really make the heart sing. Think of all the various forms of daisy like asters, with their lovely purple hues they combine very well with the red and gold blaze Heleniums and Black-eyed Susans (Rubeckia), and with heliopsis the false sunflower and dyer's chamomile too. Glorious chrysanthemums shine bronze and gold. The cone-flower family, echinacea, do their bit too along with the many lovely varieties of tickseed (coreopsis). The winter windflower, anemone blanda, gives a rainbow carpet under the trees along with autumn crocus. Late crocosmias add their orange fire amongst the red-gold of tall autumn grasses. Japanese anemones stand tall and blousy, shedding pink and white petals towards the end of the season when we get a high wind.

Autumn is a marvellously coloured season. And all these flowers are there giving their pollen to the bees and insects in exchange for the late pollination they need. Nature is very wonderful.

Garden Jobs

As the days begin to shorten in late summer, we know we are on the cusp of autumn and need to consider how we can help insects like butterflies and moths get through the coming winter.

Some garden butterfly species such as Small Tortoiseshell and Peacock overwinter as adults and will need to feed up on nectar, which they store as fat inside their bodies. Like mammals such as squirrels and hedgehogs, their metabolism will slow down in winter so they use as little energy as possible until springtime. Others like Painted Lady and Red Admiral will use the nectar to fuel their migrations to Europe and Africa – it's amazing to think that butterflies we see in our gardens in the UK may turn up in another garden hundreds of miles away!

My favourite late-summer planting style is known as Prairie planting, as many of the plants used in it are derived from the prairies of North America. Plants like goldenrod, monarda, salvia, tall daisies, phlox, rudbeckia, echinacea and helenium are all available in garden centres. They produce colourful flowers on tall spikes that you can mix with wavy grasses, giving a very naturalistic appearance that only improves as the summer goes on. These are all perennial plants, and have the advantage that invertebrates can tuck themselves down at the bases of the plants to spend the winter there.

If you've got a smaller space, or even a window box or small balcony or patio with planters, it's essential to choose plants which really give a lot of nectar so you can cram as much good into a limited area. I recommend any of the Sedums with large flat heads studded with pink flowers, such as Sedum 'Autumn Joy'. It's also hard to go wrong with lavender, salvias and veronica. Most garden centres also sell at least one variety of Sea Holly (Eryngium), but I love them all! The stem leaves are soft and green at first, but as they mature the flowers and stems turn electric blue and become spikey. The flower heads hold hundreds of tiny flowers packed with nectar which are great for insects now, and the dried flower heads look stunning on a crisp winter morning when covered in frost.

Butterflies and moths will also take sugar from fallen fruit, so remember to leave fallen fruit on the ground for them, or move it all to certain spots where the fruit can break down to release those sugars. You could even make a butterfly feeding table. In my garden I see Comma butterflies drinking sugar from fallen Rowan berries every September, so I leave them on the ground.

If you've got a slightly more shaded area with decent soil, Japanese Anemones and Thalictrum will be reaching their peak come September, and hardy geraniums can give a second late-flowering if you've dead-headed them after the first flowering earlier in the summer. Or you buy one of the long-flowering varieties like my favourite, Rozanne.

Pruning some shrubs and trees (such as apple, pear and plum trees) in late summer can help the trees, *if* you can do it without disturbing nesting birds. If you do prune now, why not simply stack the material in a quiet corner of the garden to make a place for wildlife to shelter and a potential hedgehog house? Beware chipping or burning, they will kill any caterpillars or the eggs of butterflies and moths which will be there, but if you leave the stuff around the garden at the bottom of hedges it will create a whole new space for wildlife – for free! And it follows in the footsteps of Mother Nature again.

Finally, if you have an area of long grass which you are treating as a meadow, I really advise you *not* to cut it in July or August. The caterpillars of Meadow Brown, Ringlet and Speckled Wood butterflies all feed on grass and will remain active as long as the temperatures are warm enough and this can be well into autumn. It's best if you leave the cut until early the following spring so that the butterflies and moths can survive.

Celebration

Giving Thanks is a must in every old tradition I know all around the world. Our ancestors were far more generous than us, very willing to give thanks for all the things nature gives us as well as sharing that goodness with the rest of the natural world. That's something many of us have lost but also one that many of us are working to get back. Gardening and working-with the natural world really speeds that process up.

In many magical traditions, it is customary to offer a blessing or a prayer of thanks when harvesting wild herbs. I always ask the plants I'd like to harvest, like the elder trees, if I may take some berries for my cordials, and I always listen for when the tree tells me I've taken enough. We really do all have that ability, it comes usually as a feeling, sometimes my hand sort of stops when I go to pick, little things like that, it doesn't come as blaring trumpets, nor as words. If you focus, because you want to hear (but don't get all tensed up about it either") you'll *feel* that "stop now" sensation. Take notice of it, follow it. And get used to sensing it, soon it'll be second nature for you.

I celebrate this second harvest with fire as I've said, and with a quiet little barbecue for me and Paul, and maybe a couple of other friends. It always feels a quiet time, warm and nourishing but happening within rather than the mad and exciting Padstow Obby Oss and the Morris Dancing ... but don't worry, we have more of that ecstatic fun next season!

For the fire, we each bring along a piece of wood to feed the fire from our own gardens, it doesn't matter if this is just a tiny twig, it comes from the garden you are guardian too and brings that energy to the fire. We also bring along some food to share, food we've made and containing food we've grown too, even if that's just the herbs. A nice meat pie, spiced up with your own oregano and thyme, or a curry containing your home-grown peppers, or a veggie soup from your own vegetables, they all count and they all bring the energy of the place you are guardian to.

We cook and sit and talk, maybe have a glass of beer or wine, or a nice cuppa, or some coffee. Like all places on earth are sacred, so is all the food Mother Earth provides us with, there's no such thing as "bad food" ... only badly grown food, without love, that hasn't cared for the plants or the soil.

As well as this I also celebrate by scattering seed, seed I've collected from my own plants as well as new seed to add to the diversity in the garden. Many seeds ripen and fall naturally around second harvest so I emulate and work with nature by scattering seed then myself. As I walk about, seeding, I say something like, "Thank you for these seeds, I trust you're helping me scatter them where they need to grow, and I trust you help them to grow into strong, healthy plants." It's always good to communicate with the garden spirit, s/he really doesn't appreciate being ignored ... any more than your human friends do!

Samhain

Season

Samhain is a time of opening and closing. The old ones tell us the doors of the hills open at Samhain to allow us to reconnect with the Faer Folk, always an edgy thing to do as we need to be well on our guard that we don't go all gullible. Otherworld always tests you to see if they can send you down the shop for a tin of striped paint! Tales tell of people who went to sleep for a night in a fairy cave and woke up a hundred years later. These tales have a lot more to them than the apparent top motive though, so sometimes the Rip Van Winkle sleep is a necessary part of your journey through life.

For some of us, Samhain is end of the year and so also the beginning. I'm not one of those, I follow the sun's rebirth at midwinter as my time of changing the year, but I am very involved with and love Samhain.

The word Samhain (pronounced sow-ain) comes from the Irish Gaelic word for "summer's end." At this time, our ancestors would use up or preserve the remaining perishable stores to sustain them through the cold and dark season. They also slaughtered any livestock that would be excess to feed through the winter, keeping only what they needed for new stock. The meat would be air-dried or smoked to keep through the winter. That's why Samhain is also called the third harvest, or Blood Harvest.

One of my patrons is Ceridwen, especially in her crone aspect and Samhain is her time of year. She has lots in common, for me, with Spider Woman from the North American traditions, indeed she got me to paint my first drum a north American buffalo hide on cedar wood, with a full spider image of her at the centre of her eight-sided web, with each of her eight legs on one of the eight sections. The symbolism of eight-ness wasn't lost on me.

Element

This between-time is between fire and earth, and these two go well together. It always makes me think of volcanoes – and I love volcanoes, have to keep a strong hold on myself when we've visited Mount Etna on Sicily or I'd jump down in there to explore! Not a good idea!

Altar

There is fire at the centre of Mother Earth and so yet again I give her fire on my altar in the garden. This time I make earth-fire, I dig a firepit and set the blaze in there. Always ask your garden spirit if where you've chosen is OK as fire in the earth can damage plants and roots, but your garden spirit will tell you if it's acceptable.

Plants

Herbs

One of the favourite ways we celebrate Ceridwen at Samhain is with some of her own juice, sloe gin that I make myself with the sloes from the blackthorn trees that grow near where I live. It's a delicious concoction made by steeping the sloe plums, along with good sugar (I always use dark brown sugar) for as long as you can bear to leave them, in gin. I say as long as you can bear because it really is that delicious and leaving the bottles alone to work can be hard, but it's so worth it!

Dried herbs will now be most of the order of the day in the kitchen although my sage bushes do keep going through most of our now much warmer winters since climate change has really got her wheels moving over the past twenty years. You can always use dried herbs for the tisanes you enjoy, and for herbal medicine if you do that, as well as cooking, just keep them as air-tight as you can so their freshness doesn't get lost. I do keep some out, and refresh them regularly, as a potpourri to remind me of the scents of summer, they refresh the mind and the emotions in the dark days. And sometimes I throw a handful into the woodburner to get that lovely scent into the room.

Veg

Roots, roots, roots, and all those lovely summer veg you froze. But there's also lots that stand all throughout the year in the garden too, like leeks, winter cabbages, broccoli and kale. They're all full of goodness and you can just pick what you need when you like. They all work well with roots like onions, carrots, swedes, parsnips and turnips, nothing like a dish of roast veg to pep you up on a cold day and it's so easy to make too.

As I have a small polytunnel I still have my salad veg as well. There are lots of tasty lettuces that grow well in an unheated tunnel, and there's all the peppery plants and rocket too as well as the sorrels, winter purslane and other herbs. They all do benefit from that shelter from the wind and driving, beating rain, and taste much better for that bit of shelter.

Flowers

There are no flowers in winter. Oh no? Really? Yes, there are. Some of the anemones continue flowering well into November and maybe December depending on the weather. Autumn crocuses, the gorgeous scented viburnum bodnatense, mahonia with its lovely scent, and my favourite one is Mahonia nitens 'Cabaret' with its fantastic orange flowers. There's the liriopes, and my favourite of these is Liriope muscari 'Okina' with its silver-white leaves and spikes of purple flowers. If you have acid soil then the camellias will do you proud. There's various stonecrops, cyclamens, winter pansies and sternbergia lutea, the autumn daffodil that I love, and all the nerines. The belladonna lily with its fabulous long purple or purple-green stems, topped with massive funnel-shaped, scented pink flowers is actually frost hardy although it doesn't look as though it should be, and a stunner for the Samhain season.

The hellebores are beginning to really come into their own now too. If you can manage it, the autumn cherry, Prunus × subhirtella 'Autumnalis', is a stunning winter garden tree. Its tiny white flowers open from deep pink buds on mild autumn days, and it continues to bloom sporadically throughout the winter. You can even take the wand-like branches, clustered with flowers, indoors for your celebration.

And for your pond there's the water hawthorn that gives a lovely scented display.

So no, of course there's no flowers for the Samhain season!.

Garden Jobs

Putting to Bed. Winter jobs in the garden require quite a lot of sitting on the hands, not doing too much and keeping out of the way of the plants! A big part of putting to bed is applying the muck and compost. If you get lots of muck on by Samhain, cover it with cardboard and leave well alone, it gives the worms and soil beasties the chance to move that muck well into the soil.

I always water the cardboard too. You want it to get wet and rot down as well, it was once a tree so it's got lots of goodness in it the soil will use. And once its wet it allows water to pass through it into the soil better. For the torrential rain we get for a lot of our winters nowadays it's much better that it pounds the cardboard rather than battering the soil itself – a win-win situation. And come the spring you can actually plant into that cardboard; it will be sufficiently composted and will also help the young plants.

In the wild, the job cardboard does was done mostly by the dropped leaves of plants and trees. They shelter the soil and make somewhere good for all the soil beasties to live through the winter, they don't really appreciate being battered to death by rain either. The cardboard does things in the garden. And the fallen leaves from the trees are wood too, like the cardboard, so they work-with the muck from the animals and birds that had fallen on the soil all spring, summer and autumn, and with the dead plant material to make the soil good again for everything to grow next year.

Using cardboard emulates nature and it also means we usefully dispose of all the mass of packaging we get every time we buy something!

And for all the gods' sakes don't "tidy up"! That's seriously how to kill off masses of wildlife. Remember all those species of butterflies who lay their eggs on long grass? Well those eggs haven't hatched yet so don't go cutting the grass so you kill them all. And the hollow stems of many plants are places where insects overwinter too. Piles of leaves and logs are where many beasties shelter, like our lovely hedgehogs that are yet another species under threat right now. And don't remove fallen leaves from the beds either – remember that mulch-n-cardboard, well those fallen leaves are doing the job too.

It is good to remove fallen leaves from grassy areas and meadows. Those leaves as they rot down are beginning to return the land to its natural state ... and that's forest! You and your garden spirit likely don't want that, so move the leaves and make them into leaf mould. And also ask your garden spirit to work with the spirits of the land around you to negotiate that your garden doesn't need, at the moment, to return to being forest.

I'm sure you know stories about enchanted forests ... well once upon a time, many thousands of years ago we all actually lived in enchanted forests, that's where the stories come from. Actually, Samhain is a good time to curl up in front of your fire, with a glass of sloe gin maybe, and enjoy rereading some of those old stories ...

Celebrating Samhain

I cook a couple of jacket potatoes in the altar fire for Paul and me, so I need to sit-with the fire for a good while like a couple of hours while the potatoes cook right through. Near the end of the cooking

I get a grill to put over the embers and grill some bacon on it to have with the potatoes, along with lashings of butter and cheese. If you don't eat meat you can always leave the bacon out. Paul sometimes puts a pot of baked beans to cook in the embers as well.

As I sit watching and keeping the fire, I ask the garden spirit to show me what she needs me to do both now and for the coming year. I keep a notebook with me to jot it all down.

Earth-fire feeds us, warms us, helps the plats to grow, part of the honouring is to accept the food and eat it with joy, out in the garden you're guardian to.

Altar fires can always be used for cooking. Cooking is not somehow un-sacred, in fact it's a very sacred thing to do as you accept the food nature has made for you and nourish yourself with it. There's lots of funny taboos and shibboleths that certainly don't fit with our old ways, life itself is sacred so how can any life-affirming activity be un-holy?

Samhain is that moment when autumn moves into winter and the plants know it too; they're well settled into the lessening of the light. The winter work they all do under the surface of the soil and the work of the little soil-beasties, worms, insects, microbes, and the mycorrhiza, enables the soil to be healthy and grow plants in the coming year.

Samhain is also known as Ancestor's Night or the Feast of the Dead. In the old ways we honour or ancestors and Samhain is very special time for this. The old Halloween customs and rituals like carving jack-o-lanterns and decorating the house and garden with skulls and spiders are part of this. Remember spider and Ceridwen?

We also make food offerings to the ancestors too. I leave a morsel of our fire feast out for them when we go back indoors.

All Hallows Celebration

When I can manage it, I go down to Boscastle in Cornwall for the utterly amazing All Hallows celebration. It's become very popular over the past few years – and I'm glad of that – so if you decide to go, you'll need to sort out where you're going to stay early on. It's quite as stunning as the Padstow Obby Oss and is quite overtly pagan – and I'm very glad of that too. It's well time we took back our old traditions and my friend Cassandra (the only person I know who does her tax return with her employment listed officially as "village witch"!) has taken on the job for this one and does it superbly. It goes on from early afternoon until we get thrown out of the pub that night. The pub, after the last dark processions, is a really good sing, with people from all over and everyone encouraged to join in; if you've got a song they'll ask you to sing it and help you along, and over your nervousness, by joining in. Good singers can really do that, and they never put you down. As we say in the old ways, the only time you look down on someone is when you're reaching a hand down to help them up. If you want to know more about this Google All Hallows Boscastle and it'll all come up, along with fantastic videos of previous years to whet your appetite.

Magical Gardens

Samhain is a good time to think about things that make a garden magical. It will always be about what makes your heart sing but if you've not had much exposure to the old magical ways of Britain then your store cupboard of ideas may be a bit thin. Here are some ideas I've collected together that may help inspire you to find your own way down your own garden path to the joys of magical gardening.

Magical Herbs

Belladonna – a member of the Solanaceae family it's used for journeying (some witches call this flying) and divinatory work. This is Deadly Nightshade, and called so for very good reasons, don't eat it and wash your hands after touching. Renaissance women used it to dilate their pupils and that's how it got its name as Bella Donna means 'beautiful woman'. *Please don't* do this yourself, it really is bad for you and can injure your eyes.

Henbane – is a medicinal plant used for spasms of the digestive tract and the leaf oil can be used to treat scar tissue. It's also a mild hallucinogen and so sometimes used in spirit work for speaking with the ancestors as it can transport you to alternate realities. Another member of the Solanaceae family, like belladonna, it needs to be treated with much respect.

Monkshood – one of its country names is Wolf's Bane, i.e. it will keep wolves away and so is good for protection. It's a very beautiful plant with spikes of ultramarine flowers, I love it and always have it in my garden. It's got deep associations with Hecate, moon goddess and goddess of witches, and said to have come from the foam that dripped from the fangs of her 3-headed dog, Cerberus. A legend from the Middle Ages – when the church was terrified of witchcraft – is that witches smeared it on their bodies to enable them to fly on their broomsticks. It does numb the senses, Cadfael uses it in Ellis Peter's novel "Monkshood" to help the pain of an old monk who suffers from arthritis, and it can also give a sensation of flying. An infusion or tisane of aconite can be sprinkled on ritual items during rituals to charge them with protective energy, the roots and leaves can also be burned in a ritual fire for the same purpose. I work with its energy. Never ingest it or inhale the fumes of the burning root!

Foxglove – some of the country names for foxglove are Witches' Gloves, Dead Men's Bells, Fairy's Glove, Bloody Fingers, Fairy Caps and Fairy Thimbles. It's another poisonous plant, all parts of it are poisonous. *Digitalis lanata* is a major source for the chemicals used to make a prescription drug called digoxin, that's commonly used for congestive heart failure and relieving associated fluid retention irregular heartbeat.

They both cure and kill ... very much about our relationship with otherworld, our attitudes will determine how the Faer Folk feel about us, always respect them, they're more powerful than you may think. As children we put the fairy-cap flowers on the ends of our fingers to connect us with the fairies!

Mandrake – a famous witch-plant. For me, it always brings to mind John Donne's poem that classical and folk guitarist, John Renbourn, set to music back in the 1960s, the words go, *"Go and catch a falling star, get with child a mandrake root ..."* The plant is about sex magic, about improving your sex life rather than about romance and love and partnerships so be careful how you use it.

Spirits of Place

A garden, or any green-space you love, is a haven. It's a safe space for you. It's a laboratory. And, very importantly, it's not really yours! A garden is a green-space you work with for a while as a caretaker. Those of us who work with the old ways know the responsibility and duty of care we each have to the universe and that creating a garden is part of that. We respect everything that lives there, all the wildlife and all the spirits of nature too. We always do our best to *work-with* all of these beings, seen and unseen.

Every part of the Earth is sacred. Some places have become well known, are focuses, nodes, of energy, often because many energy lines congregate there and form patterns, like at Stonehenge. But because where your house is isn't the middle of Stonehenge or Avebury doesn't mean it has no spirit of place as its guardian. Every place does.

It's a very good idea to get to know the spirit that is guardian to where you live, they all have so much to offer us but they will always wait for us to ask to get to know them, to open the door. They never get in your face.

An easy way to begin to make friends with your spirit of place is to go sit in the garden. Take a cup of tea or other drink with you, have a notebook and pen beside you, make yourself comfy in your favourite place in the garden.

Now sit quietly. Allow thoughts to drift across your mind gently, don't push for something to answer you and don't look for Steven Spielberg special effects either! Most likely the answers will come very gently not with trumpeting heralds, so stay relaxed and quiet in yourself. As one of my best teachers used to say, "Be full of expectancy but without expectations". It's very good advice if not always that easy to do!

As you sit, hearing the birds, maybe a breeze, maybe leaves rustling, just notice everything around you. A butterfly maybe comes to sit on your knee, on your book, or perhaps a bumble bee. Or a bird hops near you, or a flower catches you eye, or a leaf, or the way the wind rustles the grass. Whatever it is, and however small, just keep very still. Let your feelings flow very quietly towards what has attracted your attention. As they flow, feel something like, "Hello, I'm [say your name]. I'd like to meet the spirit of place who is guardian here where I live."

Then just wait. Observe your feelings, what images come into your mind's eye? Do you get a warm feeling inside? You may get more, and deeper, impressions. Just watch them. And allow yourself to respond to them too. But always go slowly.

Imagine you're out in the woods and a fox or a rabbit comes close to you. You don't want to frighten it away, you want the critter to stay. Often people get a sort of loving thread go out from their heart to the beastie and it looks up at you. It's noticed you, your energy, and felt you reaching to it. If you get excited then the energy will be too strong and it'll run.

It's very similar when you begin to work with spirit energy. The spirit is perfectly well aware of you, has maybe watched you for ages and you've not responded before ... now you are. The spirit doesn't yet know how friendly you really are, whether you're the sort that galumphs around trampling things or if you're careful how and where you put your energy.

Make a note of things you felt and noticed, no matter how small or if your logical mind thinks they're relevant, make note of all of it. Try just a doodle rather than neat and grammar-perfect sentences, you'll catch the drift of what you felt and saw much better with doodles. Finish your tea – I always pour the last dregs of my drink onto the ground as a thank-you offering – and say thank you as well, even though you're not sure who you're thanking or what for. Say you'll come back again soon and hope to meet with the garden spirit again. You will have met, even if you don't know it yet!

And keep your promise, go back and sit-with your garden and her/his spirit again. Give it all time and you'll find fairly quickly that you begin to recognise the feeling of your garden spirit being there. In a season or three you'll wonder how you ever managed to garden without knowing your garden spirit ...

Wildlife

When I sit in my Adirondack chair by the pond and watch dragonflies mating or laying their eggs, the water-boatmen rowing their way across the water, a sparrow "hawking" for insects over the surface or standing on a lily leaf to take a drink, and the youngling birds have a group-bath-in on the shallow place I made for them on the other side, I'm in heaven. Same when I'm at my rickety little table in the rose garden and stop writing to watch the bees, butterflies, birds, squirrels all feeding and playing around me. And occasionally a fox, stoat, badger or even polecat comes into the garden if I'm out at twilight (which I am when I can be) I'm in ecstasy. I'm so in love with the wild world and so pleased that the wild ones find the little spot of land I'm guardian to; a place where the non-human inhabitants of our Earth feel safe. That's being a sanctuary.

My gardens are always wildlife friendly. I do untidy things, don't make nice neat straight edges, don't chop down all those nasty weeds. I let the wild poppies – weeds to many folk – grow in in my garden meadows every year, they look gorgeous, and help the pollinators so I even let them grow amongst the veg along with the ubiquitous borage that the bees adore. My veg garden is proper pottager ... but it feeds me and my husband very well thus proving that neat and tidy don't necessarily mean a productive garden.

I keep lots of untidy areas too, log and stone piles that all create safe spaces for belly wrigglers as well as six and eight-legged ones to make their home. Bees, bugs, crawlers – they all have their purpose. They pollinate the flowers or aerate the soil and help to make it rich. And they all provide food for other, bigger forms of wildlife like birds.

What posh gardeners call untidy and weed-ridden – if carefully arranged along with the beauty that makes your heart sing – are much better spaces for wildlife to live and hibernate than all the manmade wildlife homes you can buy online or at the garden centre. They're much cheaper too! But remember all those folks who're trying to sell you the manmade stuff are not going to think so ... how can they when what you do stops you giving them your money?

The garden provides good housing, shelter and food for my local wildlife. And for me too. There's lots of stuff with native berries and nuts, especially now I've planted a native wildlife hedge along the north fence by next door's paddock. It includes native shrubs as well as trees, and many of them flower and some I can eat the fruit from too so we all share together. And it'll be a great windbreak to the northerly and north-east winds that are as bitter for the wildlife as they are for me. They are hardy, wildlife-friendly and can grow big and strong in your garden with very little work from you

As I'm sure you've already grasped pagans care deeply about everything non-human and we don't separate off from the non-human world as many people tend to do. I hear so many people nowadays wishing they could be more connected with the natural world, they come to me to help them and I do offer courses and trainings, many now online, that previous students have found invaluable. I hope this book will be part of that work and help you to dip your toe into the wonderful, endless pool of knowing that connecting with the non-human world brings. Gardening is certainly an excellent way to begin that. I should warn you though, it's incredibly addictive! Once you start it'll become a pillar of your life, you'll be thinking about plants and gardens, asking your garden spirit what they think about having a fountain over there, or if they'd like a hazelnut tree in the hedge. You may also find you're boring some of your friends – who haven't yet discovered the delights of gardening this way to death. Don't say you've not been warned!

Magical Gardening Ideas

A very common thing I found when I was practising as a garden designer was that clients would say something like, "I really would like to honour and learn about the Old Ways but I don't want my garden to look weird. I've got neighbours and friends who won't like it!"

That's happens a lot. People need to feel safe about "coming out" as wanting to be, thinking about, or actually being pagan. They know to do so could lose them friends, upset their children and their children's friends, even get them shunned in their neighbourhood. All unpleasant stuff – yes that kind of "religious discrimination" still happens a lot in our modern world. But it is perfectly possible to have your garden as a place where you honour the spirits and the old ways, and wildlife, but still appear reasonably normal so you don't upset the other mums in the parent/teacher group and your kids don't get jeered at and bullied because the mum is weird. You can hide your stuff so people won't realise unless they already know or you tell them and still enjoy your own private pagan garden. For goodness sakes, we pagans here in Britain have been doing that for 2000 years!

And I still do, but much less now since I became a best-selling author, that does help although it feels a bit weird to me sometimes ... I mean why does how many books I've sold somehow make me respectable in the eyes of people who laughed at me before?

There's no way for me to separate "practicing the old ways" from "gardening", I am both, I do both, both are an integral part of my life but I don't need to be ostentatious about it. There are lots of little things, like waking at dawn and coming out at dusk to mark the positions of shadows, and special places that you really only notice in the twilight times. Every garden has them, always, but you have to be looking and you have to go out in the twilight.

I was a professional garden designer for years and just about every customer I had said they wanted their garden to be a sanctuary... a preserve, a refuge from their everyday life, somewhere they could get away, felt safe, safe haven. And many of them wanted their garden to be a refuge and preserve for wildlife too, they wanted to do their bit for nature. I feel, sense, these words were a part of how they felt they good best express their need for "otherness", something more, something magical in their lives.

There are lots of simple things you can do, we've talked about them in the chapters on the Seasons, like a pollinator area with local, insect, bird and bee attracting plants. One that I do is use edible herbs that will creep and take over beds and bed edges so weeds won't be such a problem. Being edible, like arctic raspberries, they're delicious for me as well as sharing their produce with insects and birds.

As part of my gardening I can't plant or weed or cultivate the garden without doing Pagan things like thanking the spirits of the land or honouring each plant's individual spirit. But again, I don't have to make a song and dance about doing that, I can whisper or even just think it as I'm working with the plants and the soil.

I'm something of a stealth-pagan in all walks of life unless I'm supposed to be standing up and talking about it. As a garden designer I created spirit-lifting spaces without needing to tell people about things they didn't want to hear or making them uncomfortable. Before COVID-19 I always opened my garden each midsummer for the local Wildlife Trust, so people could come and enjoy, learn how I do it and see if they saw something they wanted to do as a result. I never talked about the pagan side of it although I would use the word "magic" quite often, it can be a very good and acceptable lead-in. I hope people will be able to come and do it again here.

It's never necessary to proselytize on to people when they come to look at the garden, it's enough for them to look and see. As my mum and step-mum used to say, "you can lead a horse to the water but you can't make him drink". There's nothing to be gained in standing on your soap box and shouting whatever your belief-system is, that doesn't win real converts, but looking at something you like does. That's what happens at the garden shows. I used to do the Royal Horticultural Society's Hampton Court Palace back in the 2000s show and won medals for my gardens too. People go there mostly to get ideas for their own gardens, as I used to before I began exhibiting there. And I got lots of ideas as an exhibitor too. They're mostly a friendly bunch, the gardeners who make show gardens for these shows, we always chatted during the three weeks of garden-build, shared ideas, and shared plants quite often too. That sharing is how people notice and get ideas from what you do. Example is so much better than shouting.

My Magical Garden Memories

The garden can be one of the most magical places in your life. It always has been in mine.

When I lived in a house down in Herefordshire a few years ago, I had a beautiful, expansive garden. It was home to just about every herb and veggie you can grow in the West Midlands of Britain. It held an altar for Merlin, Pan, Bridey, Ceridwen, a woodland grove, a big pool, lots of lovely shrubs and an orchard that was covered in cowslips in late spring. We also had a place for our local Faer folk who called themselves Archenlanders after the ancient British name for that part of Britain. The house was set in what had been – and still felt itself to be – the smallest kingdom in Britain, in the old tongue it was called Ergyng, or Archen, and both words mean hedgehog so I lived in the land of the hedgehog. It was very magical, surrounded by prehistoric sites, standing stones and pre-Roman sacred places. One of them was a Neolithic burial chamber made of great stone slabs, set in the hills above Herefordshire's Golden Valley and at the site of a very ancient crossroads. One of the tracks, the east-west line, is still a lane used by the locals but the north-south line has gone back to being the footpath it began life as perhaps 10,000 years ago.

Alfred Watkins, a wealthy businessman and antiquarian who lived in Hereford put forward the concept of ley lines in his 1922 book Early British Trackways. He expanded his ideas, taking them to greater depth, in The Old Straight Track in 1925. His idea of "leys" or paths traversing the British landscape from sacred place to sacred place was something I got into with my husband, Paul, in the 1970s, indeed we were on one of the first scientific surveys, called the Dragon Project, that came out with amazing results of scientifically repeatable things happening along the lines and at the sacred sites. It was fascinating. This

Neolithic tomb, called Arthur's Stone, was a point on one of the first ley lines Watkins explored. It was awesome being able to walk his line, sleep in the old tomb sometimes and work up there. I found that the hill it was at the top of was a place of Gwyn ap Nudd, one of the Old Powers I've always worked with, and of Ceridwen. Gwyn was my major Guardian while I lived at that house and brought me to the place where I now live, in sight of another of his famous hills, the Caradoc, and in the country of one of his famous human representatives, Wild Edric, an Anglo Saxon lord who fought the Normans even after Hastings and, for a short time he succeeded but then was brought under the Norman thumb. For the past near a thousand years the locals have seen him ride the Stretton Hills with the Wild Hunt – Gwyn's hounds and hunt.

My life's always been full of magic. Both my dad and mum's families were deeply involved in the old ways of Britain, and pagans, so brought me up in them too. The first magical garden I remember was at the cottage we lived in down a track on the outskirts of Clevedon in Somerset. The garden centred around an old Victoria plum tree from which dad had hung my swing, around the tree was a circle of lavender bushes and behind them a circle of old China roses, the sort that begin blooming in late April/May and continue past the first frosts. It was a little scented dell, hidden as dad had made a crooked path to it from the house (it was a big garden) so you didn't find it until you stumbled on it round a corner. I used to go down there and sit on my swing to meet with the fairies who lived in the garden. My aunts, mum's sisters who were far more "normal" used to tell dad to stop me being so silly, fortunately dad used to tell them to shut up and go away!

When we moved to Okehampton on the northern edge of Dartmoor we didn't have a garden but the family next door did. It was a beautiful old Victorian walled garden that had been just for vegetables but was now, roses and patches of grass as well.

Their daughter and I used to play there for hours and it was full of the faer folk too, she was the only other child I knew in Okehampton who knew about fairies and played with them.

When we moved from Okehampton up to the village on the edge of Exmoor mum had been dead for about three years. We now lived in an ancient thatched cottage that had once been The Green Lion, one of the nine pubs the village had a couple of hundred years before. Dad got a housekeeper to look after me so he could go to work and fairly quickly she and dad fell in love, they got married the next year. Like all step-kids and step-mums we had our ups and downs but I loved her. Vera was half Romany, and one of the old folk too as were her sisters and quite a few other folk in the village too so I grew up then surrounded by other people who all followed the old magical ways of Britain.

We had a big garden there. The land the cottage stood on was raised about 15 foot up above the road, the soil held back by a huge wall and in that wall was a space left for the old village well. It was a sacred well and to a unique saint, and the land it stood on was owned by my aunt Ida, Vera's sister. Our next door neighbour was the village midwife and herb-wife who also midwifed the dead so I learned a lot from her too. I had an uncle who was a really magical gardener, used to do biodynamic stuff long before I ever heard of it though I found out after dad died that he'd known about it as his family knew Rudolf Steiner well. Another uncle, Uncle Jack, was a woodsman – not a gamekeeper but a tree and woods man – and he taught me lots about how to be with wild animals and plants, and the old ogham tree lore. I've seen Uncle Jack call a wild hawk down to his wrist, no words or vocal calling just holding up his hand and calling with his mind, and the hawk would stoop down and land on his fist. He could call owls to and taught me how to do it.

I have quite a few friends of my generation who were brought up in the old ways too, some of them are authors and write about it too, others are artists and crafts folk, and some teach the old ways as I do. And we all of us garden. We all work-with the land where we live, asking it what it needs and wants from us, telling it what we would like and what would make our hearts sing. We've a lifetime of experience to help us work-with and negotiate with the Spirits of Place and the spirits of the plants and trees ... and now we're hoping to entice you into working that way too. We can all assure you it's enormously good fun, very rewarding and satisfying, and it really does help to make your heart sing ...

Good gardening to you all.

Practically Pagan – An Alternative Guide to...

An Alternative Guide to Cooking
Rachel Patterson

978-1-78904-379-2 (Paperback)
978-1-78904-380-8 (e-book)

An Alternative Guide to Gardening
Elen Sentier

978-1-78904-373-0 (Paperback)
978-1-78904-374-7 (e-book)

An Alternative Guide to Health & Well-being
Irisanya Moon

978-1-78904-377-8 (Paperback)
978-1-78904-378-5 (e-book)

An Alternative Guide to Planet Friendly Living
Mabh Savage

978-1-78904-445-4 (Paperback)
978-1-78904-446-1 (e-book)

MOON BOOKS

PAGANISM & SHAMANISM

What is Paganism? A religion, a spirituality, an alternative belief system, nature worship? You can find support for all these definitions (and many more) in dictionaries, encyclopaedias, and text books of religion, but subscribe to any one and the truth will evade you. Above all Paganism is a creative pursuit, an encounter with reality, an exploration of meaning and an expression of the soul. Druids, Heathens, Wiccans and others, all contribute their insights and literary riches to the Pagan tradition. Moon Books invites you to begin or to deepen your own encounter, right here, right now.

If you have enjoyed this book, why not tell other readers by posting a review on your preferred book site.

Recent bestsellers from Moon Books are:

Journey to the Dark Goddess
How to Return to Your Soul
Jane Meredith
Discover the powerful secrets of the Dark Goddess and
transform your depression, grief and pain into healing
and integration.
Paperback: 978-1-84694-677-6 ebook: 978-1-78099-223-5

Shamanic Reiki
Expanded Ways of Working with Universal Life Force Energy
Llyn Roberts, Robert Levy
Shamanism and Reiki are each powerful ways of healing; together,
their power multiplies. *Shamanic Reiki* introduces techniques to
help healers and Reiki practitioners tap ancient healing wisdom.
Paperback: 978-1-84694-037-8 ebook: 978-1-84694-650-9

Pagan Portals – The Awen Alone
Walking the Path of the Solitary Druid
Joanna van der Hoeven
An introductory guide for the solitary Druid, *The Awen Alone* will
accompany you as you explore, and seek out your own place
within the natural world.
Paperback: 978-1-78279-547-6 ebook: 978-1-78279-546-9

A Kitchen Witch's World of Magical Herbs & Plants
Rachel Patterson
A journey into the magical world of herbs and plants, filled with
magical uses, folklore, history and practical magic. By popular
writer, blogger and kitchen witch, Tansy Firedragon.
Paperback: 978-1-78279-621-3 ebook: 978-1-78279-620-6

Shaman Pathways – The Druid Shaman
Exploring the Celtic Otherworld
Danu Forest
A practical guide to Celtic shamanism with exercises and
techniques as well as traditional lore for exploring the Celtic
Otherworld.
Paperback: 978-1-78099-615-8 ebook: 978-1-78099-616-5

Traditional Witchcraft for the Woods and Forests
A Witch's Guide to the Woodland with Guided Meditations and
Pathworking
Mélusine Draco
A Witch's guide to walking alone in the woods, with guided
meditations and pathworking.
Paperback: 978-1-84694-803-9 ebook: 978-1-84694-804-6

Wild Earth, Wild Soul
A Manual for an Ecstatic Culture
Bill Pfeiffer
Imagine a nature-based culture so alive and so connected,
spreading like wildfire. This book is the first flame...
Paperback: 978-1-78099-187-0 ebook: 978-1-78099-188-7

Naming the Goddess
Trevor Greenfield
Naming the Goddess is written by over eighty adherents and
scholars of Goddess and Goddess Spirituality.
Paperback: 978-1-78279-476-9 ebook: 978-1-78279-475-2

Shapeshifting into Higher Consciousness
Heal and Transform Yourself and Our World with Ancient
Shamanic and Modern Methods
Llyn Roberts
Ancient and modern methods that you can use every day to
transform yourself and make a positive difference in the world.
Paperback: 978-1-84694-843-5 ebook: 978-1-84694-844-2

Readers of ebooks can buy or view any of these bestsellers by
clicking on the live link in the title. Most titles are published in
paperback and as an ebook. Paperbacks are available in traditional
bookshops. Both print and ebook formats are available online.

Find more titles and sign up to our readers' newsletter at
http://www.johnhuntpublishing.com/paganism
Follow us on Facebook at https://www.facebook.com/MoonBooks
and Twitter at https://twitter.com/MoonBooksJHP